Crisis Control

Solutions

What to Do When in Difficult Situations

By

Wale Oyeniyi

Table of Contents

Chapter 1: Trouble Is Natural In Life

As humans living on earth, we are bound to have one form of trouble or the other. Circumstances will always arise that will distort the normal flow of life, and we should know that God desires to make us holy and acceptable to Him in order for us not to perish than making our life easy and enjoyable. This is because holiness has an everlasting value that will make us to spend eternity with God in heaven, but temporary joy and happiness might lead us to sin which will lead us to eternal condemnation. The main reasons why children of God experience trouble and crisis sometimes is that He wants to discipline us and makes us more like Jesus Christ. These troubles can come in the form of health related problems, financial troubles, marital troubles, or even family related troubles.

Even as children of God, we are not exempted from troubles in life, but the difference in our case is that God will arise and fight our battles, and turn our troubles to tributes. That is why the bible says in the book of (Job 14:1-2),

"Man that is born of woman is of few days, and full of trouble. He comes forth like a flower, and withers, he flees like a shadow, and continue not.""

There is no man that comes to this earth and has a free ride in life without troubles and obstacles coming their way, no, not one and that is why it is written in (1 Corinthians 10:12-13)

"Therefore let anyone who thinks that he stands take heed lest he fall. No temptation has overtaken you that is not common to man. God is faithful and he will not let you be tempted beyond your strength, but with temptation, will also provide you a way of escape, that you may be able to endure it.""

That is exactly what happened in the life of Job. When trouble and temptation took total control of Job's life God gave him a way of escape and his latter days were far greater than his former days.

The bible tells us that Job was a blameless and upright man, one who feared God and turned away from evil. (Job 1:1). Because of the love and fear that Job had for God, he was highly blessed with material riches and children. Job had so many servants under his control, and he was considered the richest and greatest man in that whole region.

But just like every beloved son of God whom God has so richly blessed far above his contemporaries, there are bound to be jealousy and envy, and people that will hate and despise you because of what God have done in your life.

These types of people are not enjoying the type of divine blessing and favor that you are enjoying from God, so they are capable of doing anything to pull you down. But in the case of Job, it was the devil himself that was envious of God's abundant blessings upon the life of Job. The bible records that,

"There was a day when the sons of God came to present themselves before the

Lord, and Satan also came among them" - (Job 1:6).

The devil was not invited, and just like the interloper and fraud that he was, he sneaked in among the children of God to present himself to God, but only for the purpose of hurting Job. When God saw Satan, he asked,

"Whence have you come? And Satan answered, from going to and fro on the earth, and from walking up and down on it" - (Job 1:7).

The devil has no direction and no bearing, he is a liar and a trouble maker looking for where to cause trouble, and that is why the bible tells us that He moves about like a roaring lion looking for whom to devour. But as children of God, we will never be his victims in Jesus name. Amen.

"And the Lord said to Satan, Have you considered my servant Job, that there is none like him on the earth, a blameless and upright man, who fears God and turns away from evil?" - (Job 1:8)

God was proud of Job, because despite his abundant riches, he was still serving God faithfully, and his ways were upright and righteous before God.

"Then Satan answered the Lord, Does Job fear God for nothing? Hast thou not built a hedge about him and his house and that he has, on every side? Thou hast blessed the works of his hand, and his possessions have increased in the land. But put forth thy hand now, and touch all that he has, and he will curse thee to thy face." - (Job 1:9-11)

Satan was doing everything possible to instigate God against Job, by making it look like Job feared God and lived an upright life because of the abundant blessings that God has given to Job. But God is a God of infinite wisdom and knowledge, a God that knows the end from the beginning and a God that rules in the affairs of men. So He knew that no matter what Satan planned to do to Job, Job would never stop loving and serving God.

"And the Lord said to Satan, Behold, all that he has is in your power, only upon himself do not put forth your hand" - (Job 1:12).

This shows us that the devil has no power over us, and all the devices of the enemy against our life will come to nothing, but for our sins and transgressions that open up room for the evil ones to trouble us, and sometimes for God's name to be glorified through our victories over our enemies. From that moment onwards, the life of Job took a negative turn, everything that he has ever owned was taken from him, bad news, evil and calamity became the order of the day.

For the bible records in (Job 1:13-19) that in one day Job lost all his oxen and asses and all his servants killed by thieves, his sheep was consumed by fire from heaven and all his children were killed by a great wind that came from the wilderness.

At that point, Job was left with nothing. All that he had ever worked for were destroyed in one day. But Job showed his complete faith and love for

God, in that he didn't despair and blame God for all the calamities that befell him.

In (Job 1:20) the bible says,

"Then Job arose, and rent his robe, and shaved his head, and fell upon the ground, and worshipped. And he said, "Naked I came from my mother's womb, and naked shall I return; the Lord gave, and the Lord has taken away; blessed be the name of the Lord."

Truthfully, Satan never expected Job to act this way, he expected Job to break down and become disillusioned, and cursed God for all the troubles that befell him in one day, but instead Job humbled himself before God, worshipped and committed everything into the hands of God.

So it is in our own lives, when trouble and problems of life overwhelm us, our enemies expect us to turn our back against God and seek to solve our problems our own way, but if we commit everything into the hands of God and trust him to fight for us, he will turn our troubles around and give us supernatural victory.

When trouble comes into the life of a child of God, and when it seems the situation is dicey, do what the word of God says in (Philippians 4:6-7),

"Have no anxiety about anything, but in everything by prayer and supplication with thanksgiving let your request be made known to God. And the peace of God, which passes all understanding, will keep your hearts and your mind in Christ Jesus."

So Job held on strongly to the faith he had in God, and persevered in faith to overcome all the crisis and trouble that the devil brought to his life, even his friends that were not very supportive in the time of his trouble and challenges, Job didn't keep offence, but rather he prayed for them.

In (Job 42:10-12) the bible says,

"And the Lord restored the fortunes of Job, when he prayed for his friends; and the Lord gave Job twice as much as he had

before. Then came to him all his brothers and sisters, all who had known him before, and ate bread with him in his house, and they showed him sympathy and comforted him for all the evil that the Lord has brought upon him, and each of them gave him a piece of money, and a ring of gold. And the Lord blessed the latter days of Job more than the beginning."

Some Major Lessons To Be Learnt By The Troubles And Life Of Job

- **Good And Righteous People Are Exposed To Temptation And Affliction**

If you take a good look at the beginning of the book of Job, you will find that the bible says,

"There was a man in the land of Uz, whose name was Job; and that man was blameless and upright, one who

feared God, and turned away from evil." - (Job 1:1)

Job's troubles didn't come about due to his sinful nature, or a major transgression in his life, no, not at all; in fact Job was so righteous he was considered blameless. The truth is that, Job's troubles, sufferings and tribulations came because Job was very righteous and he feared God.

So sometimes, the enemy can afflict God's children and bring monumental trouble into their lives and family because they love God so much and keep to His status, but just like in the case of Job, God can allow it to happen in order to see how faithful we are and to bring glory to his name when we turn out victorious.

So we need to be aware that all afflictions and trouble is not due to sin and transgression, but it can be temptations and trials to take us to a higher spiritual level in the service of God, just like in the case of Job.

- ## God's Love And Presence Is Always With Us

Sometimes when serious trouble befalls us, and when we look everywhere and it seems like there is no hope, then we start thinking that even God has abandoned us, and that his divine presence is no longer with us.

But that is not true, though God might be silent for a while, but His divine presence never lives his children. For His word says in (Deuteronomy 31:6),

> ***"Be strong and of good courage, do not fear or be in dread of them; for it is the Lord who goes with you, he will not fail you or forsake you."***

So when you are in crisis and trouble times, don't let the enemy deceive you that God has abandoned you, that his presence has left you and that you are now completely on your own, that is a big lie from the pit of hell, because God's promises never fail, hold on to Him strongly in times of trouble and commit everything unto His able and caring hands.

In the case of Job, he experienced complete silence from God in times of his troubles and sufferings, to the point that Job asked God "WHY" several times, but he got no answer from God, and when his sufferings became strong and unbearable, Job sought the face of God so that he can personally plead his innocent case before God.

It became unbearable at a point that Job wrote,

"Behold, I go forward, but He is not there and backward but I can't perceive Him. On the left hand, I seek Him, but can't behold him. I turn to the right hand, but I can't see him. But he knows the way that I take; when he has tried me, I shall come forth as gold." - (Job 23:8-10)

Job looked for God everywhere, but he couldn't find Him, but he made a statement of truth showing that he knows that God's presence has not left him, Job said,

"But He knows the way that I take; when He has tried me, I shall come forth as gold." - (Job 23:10)

So job was very certain that despite how hard and dreadful his situation was, and how the sufferings that fell upon him has completely destroyed everything he ever labored for, God's presence was still with him, in fact God knows every step that he took and every thought that came out from his mind.

So when you are in times of crisis, don't ever believe that God has abandoned you, and that his presence has left you, on the contrary brethren, hold on strong, because God will never leave you nor forsake you.

- **Faithfully Hold On To God**

A lot of people are tempted to lose hope in God in times of crises and troubles, especially when the problem becomes persistent and unbearable. At this point, and just because they think God has abandoned them, they start searching for the solution to their problems in different ways, even to the point of abandoning God's ways and promises.

But Job never did that, and for a man that lost so much in one day, and got afflicted with sickness, Job stood firm and held on faithfully to God.

So be rest assured that no matter what you are passing through right now, and no matter how it looks like the crisis you are passing through will consume you, the truth is those pictures of hopelessness and despair is being painted by the devil to discourage you from putting all your hope and trust in the Lord where your salvation and freedom truly is.

Put your hope and trust in the Lord today, hold on strongly to Him and all your troubles will pass away.

- ## **Humble Yourself, Fear God And Avoid Sin**

The period of crisis and trouble should be a time of humility, and fear of God. We should check the types of statements that we make. We should humble ourselves and give God thanks for being alive, reverence and praise his Holy name even in the midst of crises and troubles.

In the case of Job, he put the fear of the Lord and humility at the forefront of everything he did, and Job said,

> *"Behold, the fear of the Lord, that is wisdom, and to turn away from evil is understanding." - (Job 28:28)*

- ## **Family, Friends And Loved Ones May Abandon**

When crisis comes into our lives, and the troubles we face become too strong, and with no solution in sight, the people that we really expect to stand by us and give us spiritual and moral support may abandon us, in fact in some worst case scenario, they will even become the ones to discourage you and make you feel miserable about your condition.

That was exactly the case of Job, because the people he considered his best friends where even the ones making his life more miserable instead of using soothing and encouraging words to alleviate his sufferings.

In (Job 16:2), Job called them,

"I have heard many such things; miserable comforters are you all."

So when the people you expect to show you love and encouragement in the time of trouble end up being the ones mocking you and making you feel miserable, don't despair or be discouraged, for though family, friends and loved ones may fail you, but God will stand firm to give you an expected end.

Despite what Job was going through, even in the peak of his sufferings and tribulations Job knew where his hope and trust lie. Job had an unshakable faith in God to vindicate and deliver him.

That is why in (Job 19:25-27), Job said,

"For I know that my Redeemer lives, and at last He will stand upon the earth, and after my skin has been thus destroyed, then from my flesh I shall see God. Whom I shall see on my side, and my eyes shall behold, and not another. My heart faints within me."

Job had faith and held on to his Redeemer even when everyone else left him, and that should be our attitude when we are going through difficult and challenging situations in life.

- **Don't Keep Offence, And Forgive All That Hurts You**

When trouble comes, people that have low understanding of what you are going through and how God works will abandon, or even say some very bad things about you that will make you more miserable, but don't keep offence or hold grudges, but pray for them and forgive them. For out of your forgiving those who hurt you will God Himself forgive you and deliver you from all the suffering and afflictions that you are going through.

In the case of Job, he forgave his friends and prayed for them, and the bible says in (Job 42:10),

"And the Lord restored the fortunes of Job, when he had prayed for his friends and the Lord gave Job twice as much as he has before."

Most situations in our life is nothing but test and temptation, and the way you handle it, will to a large extent determine the level of victory that you will achieve.

The bible records that God,

"blessed the latter days of Job more than his beginning" - (Job 40:12).

- **We Need To Comfort And Encourage People In Trouble**

As children of God, we need to know that our duty is to comfort and encourage those that are going through sufferings and trouble times, instead of claiming self-righteousness and assuming that their problems came about due to sin or transgression.

We should not judge others, so that God in His anger will not judge us. Just as it is in the case of Job's friends, because the truth was that, at that critical point in Job's life, all he needed was words of edification and encouragement, and not words of chastisement and rebuke.

So whenever we meet people that are grieving and suffering, we should show the love of God in us by being comforters and not judges, we should pray for people in trouble and leave everything in the hands of God.

That was why God was angry with Job's friends because they spoke words of rebuke instead of love, edification and encouragement when their friend, Job was in trouble.

In (Job 42:7) the bible says,

> ***"After the Lord has spoken these words to Job, the Lord said to Eliphaz the Temanite, my wrath is kindled against you and against your two friends; for you have not spoken of me what is right, as my servant Job has. Now therefore take seven bulls and seven rams, and go to my servant Job, and offer up for yourself burnt offering, and my servant Job shall pray for you, for I will accept his prayers not to deal with you according to your folly, for you have not spoken of me what is***

right, as my servant Job has." - (Job 42:7-8)

So we need to be very careful what we say to people going through crisis and trouble, in order not to incur the wrath of God.

- **Trouble And Crises Shows How Little Our Life Is**

The life that we live is not our own, and we have no power to control the air that we breath and all these is proven in times of crisis and trouble. So no one should boast in their strength, or assume that they have the power to make things happen because they are strong, healthy and trouble free at the moment.

But rather, we should humble ourselves and give due respect and praise to God who made heaven and earth and all that are in them, for only him is in complete control of our life and everything that we have.

In (Psalms 8:4-6),

"What is man, that thou are mindful of him? And the son of man, that thou visitest him. For thou has made him a little lower than the angel, and had crowned him with glory and honor. Thou made him to have dominion over thy works of thy hands; thou hast put all things under his feet."

So man's life is nothing, but God in His love and mercy made man to have dominion on earth and gave man glory and honor, but we should not lose sight of who our lives truly belongs to and start boasting in our own strength and wisdom.

In (James 4:14) the bible says,

"Whereas you do not know about tomorrow. What is your life, for you are a mist that appears for a little time and then vanishes."

So crisis and trouble remind us that the life we are living does not belong to us, but to

God who has the power to control all things.

How To React In Times Of Crisis And Trouble

As children of God, and people who believe in the resurrection power of Jesus Christ, when crisis and trouble come into our life or family, we should first of all put all our hope and trust in God, and in the victory that Christ has obtained for us on the cross of Calvary when He shed his blood for us.

Though the situation that we are going through might be too strong and overwhelming for us, but we should not give up because the victory of Jesus on the cross and the promises of God has given us the assurance that no matter what we are going through we will come out victorious to the glory of God.

Jesus promised us in (John 16:33),

"These things I have spoken to you, that in me you may have peace. In the world you

will have tribulation; but be of good cheer, I have overcome the world."

Know that trouble will come. The bible makes it very clear that trouble will always arise, but that if we persevere and have faith in God, that situation will make us stronger and better.

In (1 Peter 5:10),

"And the God of all grace, who called you to his eternal glory in Christ, after you have suffered a little while, will himself restore you and make you strong, firm and steadfast ."

So know that trouble will come because of the nature of the sinful world that we live in, but that victory is guaranteed in Christ, we need to comport ourselves and have a mind of victory because we shall surely overcome.

Develop a positive mindset in times of trouble. The type of positive spiritual mindset that we develop during the time of trouble determines the degree of victory we enjoy, how quickly the victory will come, and the level of blessing that we enjoy.

So we need to be grounded spiritually and have a positive spiritual mindset when crisis and trouble come into our life.

Look for the lessons and opportunities in the trouble. Every challenge that we face comes with its peculiar lessons to learn and opportunities to make positive changes in our lives, and amend any failures and mistakes that we made in our lives before.

So react positively by looking out for the lessons to be learnt in times of trouble, and make sure that the lessons learnt are used to refine and redirect your life to the better you that you desire.

The time of trouble is a great time to see God's hand in your life. Time of trouble is great time to know the purpose of God in our lives, it is good time to know why he allowed trouble to come into our life in the first place. Though not by questioning God and arrogantly asking why you, but to humbly commit everything into his hands and let his will be done concerning your situation.

See that God is using the situation to strengthen you, and to bring out the best in you. God's presence is with us in whatever we are passing through, and if you humbly ask him in prayer and fasting, you will discover the hand of God in times of trouble and the way out of your trouble.

Put all your trust on God. As a child of God trouble will come, even as Jesus rightly told us that tribulations will come, but when it comes, we should not panic or despair, but we should put all our trust in God and have faith that He is more than capable of taking absolutely control of whatever situation you are passing through.

The word of God has told us exactly how to commit everything into his hand in (Philippians 4:6 which) says,

"Do not be anxious about anything, but in everything by prayer and supplication and thanks giving let your request be made known to God."

There is nothing that God can't do, so cast all your cares on God because God loves you and cares for you.

Don't forget the power of God to do the impossible. Two of the greatest mistakes we can make in times of trouble and crises is to blame God why he allowed such problem to come into our lives in the very first place and to believe that God is not capable of handling the situation, thereby taking it upon ourselves to seek for solution outside God's presence.

These two mistakes can be very costly, and it will open us up to more manipulation and control to the evil powers of the enemy.

First you should know that God is not a wicked God, and that He is not the author of crisis and confusion. God will not gain anything from hurting you, or bringing trouble into your life, but when trouble comes, as it will happen to all men on earth, know and believe that the God you serve is more than powerful and capable to deliver you and make a way of escape for you.

The truth is that, it can be frustrating when we are facing crisis and trouble, but at no point should we lose hope in the ability of God to deliver us at His appointed time, and we should never blame God, because that will withhold the hand of God from manifesting quickly in your situation.

So even if you are facing financial crisis, marital crisis, health related crisis, or no matter any trouble or loss you are going through, just have faith in God and believe in His power to heal, deliver and set you free.

The word of God says in (Jeremiah 32:27),

"Behold, I am the Lord, the God of all flesh; is there anything too hard for me?"

And the honest answer to this is absolutely nothing. So no matter what the situation is, it is not hard or impossible for God to handle. So let Him handle it.

He loves you and wants the best for you and that is why He says,

"For I know the plans that I have for you, says the Lord, plans for welfare and not evil, to give you a future and a hope. Then you will call upon me and come and pray, and I will hear you. You will seek me and find me when you seek me with your whole heart." - (Jeremiah 29:11-13)

This is God speaking, so what are you waiting for?

Constantly read and meditate on God's word. The word of God is powerful, it is soothing and has the capacity to heal you and provide all the solutions and comfort you need in times of crisis and trouble.

The word of God is spirit and life, and in (2 Timothy 3:16-17) it is written,

"All scripture is breathed out by God and profitable for teaching, for reproof, for correction, and for training in righteousness, that the men of God may be competent, equipped for every good work."

So if all scriptures are breathed out by God and are profitable, then it has the spirit of God living in it, so harness the profit in the word of God and allow His Spirit to take over your trouble and deliver for you the victory that you desire.

A lot of people suffer and struggle through crisis and trouble because of poor knowledge of God's word and because they have a very weak spiritual foundation, no wonder God Himself said, "My people perish for lack of knowledge."

But if you read the word of God constantly, meditate on it and act according to the promises of God, then there is no crisis and trouble that you can't overcome and come out stronger and victorious. In (Romans 10:17) the word of God says,

"So then, faith comes by hearing, and hearing by the word of God. So whenever you are in crisis, or faced by a serious trouble, you should make the word of God your refuge because in it you will find direction, peace, comfort and the solution to your problems."

Pray and have faith in God that He will answer you. The truth is that when we are going through crisis, and when the troubles of life become too strong and unbearable, praying becomes a little hard.

We tend to get frustrated and loose hope after we had prayed for some time and it seems like all our prayers are not being answered, but that is the best time to pray more and the prayer might not necessarily be long, a prayer done in faith like this might be enough when you are feeling tired and overwhelmed. *"Father I thank you for the gift of life. I praise your Holy name because I know that you are bigger than my situation, and that you are in total control of my situation. So Father let your will be done in Jesus name. Amen."*

Always pray in faith believing that you have received what you prayed for and God will answer your prayers.

It is written,

"Truly, I say to you, whoever says to this mountain, 'be taken up and cast into the

sea,' and does not doubt in his heart, but believes what he says will come to pass, it will be done for him. Therefore I tell you, whatever you ask in prayer, believe that you have received it, and it will be yours."
- (Mark 11:23-24)

So prayers done in faith can move mountains, and they have the capacity to turn your situation around and restore wholeness back to your life, start now to use this time tested and very powerful weapon and your life will forever be turned around.

Give thanks always. Yes, I know this might sound a little too hard for some people, especially people that are not so grounded in the ways and workings of God.

When we look all around us, and all we see is crisis, trouble, hopelessness and despair, it becomes very hard, or almost impossible to give God thanks. But if you understand how God really operates, then you will know that when situations overwhelms you, and when all hope seems lost, that is actually the best time to give thanks to God for all He has done in your life.

Yes, you might be tempted to ask about all the things that He has done that you need to give thanks for because you may be sick, suffering from chronic poverty and besieged by debt, the marital crisis you are facing might have gone out of control, or the evil attack of your enemies has rendered you useless, so you see nothing to give thanks for.

The bible says,

"Rejoice always, pray without ceasing, give thanks in all circumstances; for this is the will of God in Christ Jesus for you." - (1 Thessalonians 5:16-18)

It is very important to be in the attitude of prayer and thanksgiving when we are facing crisis and trouble because that is the only way to move the hands of God to respond in our situation and fight our battles. God will never respond to a grumbling heart, or a heart that blames Him and refuses to give Him thanks for at least being alive to behold that new day.

> ***"Blessed is the man who remains steadfast under trial, for when he has stood the test he will receive the crown of life, which God has promised to those who love Him." - (James 1:12)***

So give God thanks in all situations, praise and exalt His Holy name because only God has the power to deliver you from all your troubles.

> ***"Count it all joy, my brothers, when you meet trials of various kinds, for you know that the testing of your faith produces steadfastness. And let steadfastness have its full effect, that you may be perfect and complete, lacking in nothing." - (James 1:2-4)***

Prayer Points

Father, I thank you for the gift of life, I praise and exalt you holy name, because you are the God that sees the end from the very beginning.

Father, I thank you for the situation in my life right now, give me the grace to rejoice and pray to you always despite my situation, for in you there is healing and restoration and in obedience to your word in (1 Thessalonians 5:16-18) which says

"Rejoice always, pray without ceasing, give thanks in all circumstances; for this is the will of God in Christ Jesus for you."

Thank you Father, in Jesus name I pray. Amen.

Father, your word said that,

"Man that is born of woman is of few days, and full of trouble. He comes forth like a flower, and withers, he flees like a shadow, and continue not" - (Job 14:1-2)

So Father, I commit my life into your able hand, guide and protect me all the days of life against crisis and trouble and give me the grace to live a life of peace and prosperity. In Jesus name I pray. Amen.

It is written in (1 Corinthians 10:13) that,

"No temptation has overtaken you that is not common to man. God is faithful and he will not let you be tempted beyond your strength, but with temptation, will also provide you a way of escape, that you may be able to endure it."

So father, in the name Jesus I pray for the grace to receive strength and escape route over all my life challenges in Jesus name. Amen.

It is written in (Philippians 4:6-7),

"Have no anxiety about anything, but in everything by prayer and supplication with thanksgiving let your request be made known to God. And the peace of God, which passes all understanding, will keep your hearts and your mind in Christ Jesus."

So Father, in the name of Jesus, I make request that from today all the crises and trouble in my life cease to exist by fire in Jesus name. Amen.

(Job 42:12), it is written,

"And the Lord blessed the latter days of Job more than the beginning."

Father, I pray in the name of Jesus to receive double restoration and double blessing for all that was lost in times of crisis and trouble in the name of Jesus. Amen.

Father, I pray for the strength, courage and faith to confront all the challenges in my life and come out victorious.

The faith to believe and hold on strongly to you in times of crisis and trouble, because I know that you will not leave me nor forsake me. Just as you promised in (Deuteronomy 31:6),

"Be strong and of good courage, do not fear or be in dread of them; for it is the Lord who Goes with you, he will not fail you or forsake you." Amen.

Thank you Father, for the blood that your Son Jesus shed for me on the cross of Calvary to redeem me and overcome all the crisis and trouble in my life, and thank you for the joy and peace in my life just as your Son Jesus promised me in (John 16:33),

"These things I have spoken to you, that in me you may have peace. In the world you will have tribulation; but be of good cheer, I have overcome the world." Amen.

Father, I thank you for the situation in my life right now.

Father, I trust and believe in you, and I know that the situation my life will work out for my own good. This I know because your word says,

"Count it all joy, my brothers, when you meet trials of various kinds, for you know that the testing of your faith produces steadfastness. And let steadfastness have its full effect, that you may be perfect and complete, lacking in nothing." - (James 1:2-4)

Thank you Father because I know I will come out better, stronger and lacking nothing in Jesus name. Amen.

It is written,

"Truly, I say to you, whoever says to this mountain, 'be taken up and cast into the sea,' and does not doubt in his heart, but believes what he says will come to pass, it will be done for him. Therefore I tell you, whatever you ask in prayer, believe that you have received it, and it will be yours."
- (Mark 11:23-24)

Father, I make all my prayers in faith and conviction of heart that you have already answered me and that all the crises and troubles in my life has been defeated by fire in Jesus name. Amen.

Chapter 2: The Hidden Blessings In The Storm

Storms of life, crisis and trouble will come into the life of a child of God from time to time, but the way we manage it, and the attitude we employ in time of trouble will determine if we are going to come out of it victorious and with blessings, or if we are going to be defeated by the storms we face. It is written,

"Blessed is the man who remains steadfast under trial, for when he has stood the test he will receive the crown of life, which God has promised to those who love him." - (James 1:12)

And in (Hebrew 12:11) the bible says,

"Now no chastening for the present seems to be joyous, but grievous; nevertheless afterward it yields the peaceable fruit of righteousness unto them which are exercised thereby."

With a positive attitude and complete trust in God, the storms of life will not defeat us, but rather it will refine us and make us come out wiser, stronger and with more faith in God.

In the peak of Job's sufferings, and even when his skin had been eaten up, Job knew that he would receive a blessing and be uplifted after the storm. So Job said,

"Behold, I go forward, but He is not there and backward but I can't perceive Him. On the left hand, I seek Him, but can't behold him. I turn to the right hand, but I can't see him. But he knows the way that I take; when he has tried me, I shall come forth as gold." - (Job 23:8-10)

Even our Lord and Savior Jesus Christ passed through trials and temptations in the wilderness when He was tempted by the devil, but He stood firm and relied on the words and promises of God, and at the end He came out stronger and the name of God glorified.

We should be aware of the devices of the devil, and that most of the storms in our life is caused by him, and his ultimate aim, is to give us so much trouble and tribulation so that we turn our backs on God, or believe that God does not care about us and whatever we are going through.

There are some spiritual blessing to be gained from crisis and trouble.

Grace

"My grace is sufficient for you, for my power is made perfect in weakness." - (2 Corinthians 12:9)

God makes His grace abundant in times of trouble when we commit the problem into His hands and allow Him to take total control of the situation.

The grace of God and experience we get in times of trouble strengthens and edifies us to the extent that nothing we face in life will ever scare us. For the bible says that,

"In all things God works for the good of those who love him, who have been called

according to His purpose." - (Romans 8:28)

God on his own will not send you trouble, or make you go through crisis, but when they come, which they will because it is part of the sinful and imperfect world that we live in, God will bless you with His grace to overcome them and come out in joy and victory.

The bible tells us that the blessings and gift of the Lord is without repentance, so when God blesses you with his Grace in times of trouble, it stays with you forever and makes you a carrier of God's divine grace.

Multiplication And Abundance After Crisis

Times of crisis and troubles are time of refinement, though it comes with pain, trial, loss and suffering, but when we commit everything to the hand of God, trust Him and have absolute faith that He is capable to deliver us from all the trouble we are into, He will bless us abundantly and multiply us when the crisis and trouble are over.

In the case of Job, the devil made sure he lost everything he had ever acquired including his children, and even afflicted Job with a deadly sickness, but in all things that happened to Job, he never forsook his God or blame God for the calamity which befell him. In fact Job was still praising God and declaring how powerful his love and goodness was.

"And the Lord restored the fortunes of Job, when he had prayed for his friends, and the Lord gave Job twice as much as he had before." - (Job 42:10)

The eyes of the Lord is on you when you are passing through any situation, and no matter how hard and bad the situation is right now, hold on to God in faith, because he wants you to learn from that situation and receive the abundant blessing and multiplication that he has in store for you. When you are going through crisis and troubles you not only lose property and finance in the quest of searching for solution especially for those going through serious health challenges, but you lose friends, and even some family members may abandon you in times of need. In the case of Job, at the peak of his suffering his brothers and sisters were nowhere to be found, but when God restored him and multiply him in double fold, everyone returned to him, even those that had known and forgotten about him.

In (Job 42:11-12) the bible says,

"Then came to him all his brothers and sisters and all who had known him before, and ate bread with him in his house, and they showed him sympathy and comforted him for all the evil that God has brought upon him, and each of them gave him a piece of money, and a ring of gold. And the Lord blessed the latter days of Job more than his beginning."

They ate and drank with him and gave him gifts, all because the hand of God was with him. So when God blesses you, He causes others to bless you too even those that had known you and forgotten you will return and bless you. Don't despair, don't lose hope, look out and wait for the blessing that comes after the storm, for your Redeemer will surely bring it to pass.

The Blessing Of Perseverance

The storms of life refine us and teach perseverance, and the bible tells us in (James 1:12) that,

> ***"Blessed is the man who endures trials, for when he had stood the test he will receive the crown of life which God has promised to those who love him."***

When we are going through the storm of life we should endeavor to persevere and remain focused to the end because there is a reward, and that reward is the blessing that God has graciously kept for those that love Him and believe that only He is their Lord and Savior.

In (Hebrews 10:35-36) we are advised not to,

> ***"Therefore do not throw away your confidence, which has great reward. For you have need of endurance, so that you***

may do the will of God and receive what was promised."

God blesses us with the spirit of perseverance and with the gift of perseverance, there is no storm or trouble that life will ever throw at us that will move us, or make us forgot that God is our source and our ever present help in times of need.

The truth is that every time we go through a storm, there is a corresponding blessing waiting for us if we persevere to the end because God has a purpose for allowing us pass through storms of life, and mainly that purpose is to strengthen us, increase our faith in Him, refine us, and make us draw closer to God. So don't place your eyes on the storm you are facing, but put your eyes and complete focus on God and in the end he will bless and reward you abundantly. In Isaiah 41:10 the word of God says,

"Fear not, for I am with you, be not be dismayed, for I am your God; I will strengthen you, I will uphold you with my victorious right hand."

God is telling you that you have absolutely nothing to fear when you are passing through the storm of life, that His presence is ever constant with you and with Him victory and blessing is assured.

The Blessing Of Fearlessness And Faith

Fear is one of the main things that makes us vulnerable and gives the devil the room to come into our life and cause all types of trouble. That is one of the reasons why the bible talks so much about fear, and why we need not to give in into fear no matter what we are going through.

> ***"The fear of man lays a snare, but whoever trust in the Lord is safe." - (Proverbs 29:25)***

God so much dislike fear because He knows the negative consequence of fear in the life of any believer that is why He said,

> ***"Fear not, for I am with you, be not be dismayed, for I am your God; I will strengthen you, I will help you, I will***

uphold you with my righteous right hand." - (Isaiah 41:10)

What a great and reassuring promise from God and it is one of these promises of God against fear that make us strong and courageous in times of crisis and trouble.

And when we are faithful and persevere to the end, God blesses us with a spirit of fearlessness, and when we gain the blessing of fearlessness after overcoming the storms of life, there is nothing that the enemy will do that will scare us. In (Proverbs 28:1) the bible says that,

"The wicked flee when no one pursues, but the righteous are bold as a lion."

When the storm of life has tested your faith in God, and you have won the battles of life, you will receive the divine faith by God.

"For by grace you have been saved through faith. And this is not your own doing; it is the gift of God not as a result of works, so that no one may boast." - (Ephesians 2:8-9)

Prayer Points

It is written,

"Blessed is the man who remains steadfast under trial, for when he has stood the test he will receive the crown of life, which God has promised to those who love him." - (James 1:12)

Father, I thank you for all the benefits that you have given me, and I pray for the strength and grace to remain steadfast under trial, so that at the end I will receive the blessing of the crown of life in Jesus name. Amen.

It is written,

"But he knows the way that I take; when he has tried me, I shall come forth as gold." - (Job 23:10)

Father, I thank you for your goodness in my life, I praise you great name for you are God that sees the end from the beginning. I thank you for the trials in my life will not consume me, but it shall refine me and make me come out as gold in Jesus name. Amen.

Father, you said that,

"My grace is sufficient for you, for my power is made perfect in weakness." - (2 Corinthians 12:9)

So Father, I pray for the blessing of grace upon my life, and for your power to manifest in my life in times of trial in Jesus name.

In (Job 42:12) the bible says,

"And the Lord blessed the latter days of Job more than his beginning."

Father, my God, king of glory, the all-knowing God, I pray today that for everything that I lost in times of trial, for you to mercifully replenish me and bless my latter days more than my beginning in Jesus name. Amen.

Father, your word says in (Hebrews 10:35-36) that,

"Therefore do not throw away your confidence, which has great reward. For you have need of endurance, so that you

may do the will of God and receive what was promised."

Jehovah king of glory, I bless your holy name and I give you thanks. Father, I humbly ask for the confidence to endure to the end, to do your will and receive all the magnificent promises that you promised those that love you, in Jesus name. Amen.

Father, you said in (Isaiah 41:10),

"Fear not, for I am with you, be not be dismayed, for I am your God; I will strengthen you, I will uphold you with my victorious right hand."

So Father, I reject the spirit of fear, and I pray for the blessing of divine faith. Give me the kind of faith that conquers all challenges and defeats every storm in life in Jesus name. Amen.

It is written that,

"The fear of man lays a snare, but whoever trust in the Lord is safe."* - *(Proverbs 29:25)

So Father, today I run into the safety of your sanctuary, and I rebuke every form of fear that has caused a snare in my life. Bless me father with the spirit of boldness and fearlessness in Jesus name. Amen.

It is written in (Proverbs 28:1) that,

"The wicked flee when no one pursues, but the righteous are bold as a lion."

So Father, give me the grace to be righteous in your sight, and endow me with boldness like a lion, so that I can trample and devour all the challenges that come before me in Jesus name. Amen.

Father, I thank you for I know that you have answered all my prayers. I know this for your word said,

"Whatever you ask in prayer, believe that you have received it, and it will be yours."
- (Mark 11:24)

Thank you Father, in Jesus name, Amen.

Chapter 3: Don't Listen To Discouragement In Pursuit Of Your Inspired Goal

There are times in our lives when we have a set goal and objective, and a God-driven purpose that we are passionate about. And this goal and purpose in our life might be for personal advancement or for the advancement of God's kingdom, and then things or people come out with a subtle and malicious intent to discourage, derail and even destroy that goal or purpose. We see these types of things in our lives every time or even in our immediate environment, where friends or even well-known enemies try to discourage us, or hinder the move of God in our lives.

A typical case study was the story of Nehemiah. He was one the Jews that were taken into captivity when Jerusalem was captured and destroyed, but the love, passion and dedication he has for the things of God never departed from him. So one day some Jews came from Judah, and out of his burning desire for the things of God, he enquired from them about the Jews in Jerusalem and how the city was presently, and they told him that Jerusalem and everything in it had been burnt by fire.

The bad news got Nehemiah very sad, and in (Nehemiah 1:4) it said,

"When I heard these words I sat down and wept, and mourned for days; and I continued fasting and praying before the God of heaven."

From that day on, a burning desire and zeal came upon Nehemiah to see that the walls of Jerusalem and its gates were repaired, and that became his goal to the point that he was no longer finding any joy and happiness doing the king's work because he was a cupbearer to the king.

The prayer and fasting of Nehemiah made the king to notice his sad countenance, for it is written.

"In the month of Nisan, in the twentieth year of king Artaxerxes, when wine was brought before him, I took up the wine and gave to the king. Now I had not been sad in his presence." - (Nehemiah 2:1)

The truth is that, Nehemiah had been coming into the king's presence for long, and the kings of those days were so powerful and godlike for them to notice if you are happy or sad, especially for a slave like Nehemiah, so it takes the special favor of God for the king to notice his mood and speak kindly to him.

In (Nehemiah 2:2) the bible says,

"And the king said to me, why is your face sad, seeing that you are not sick? This is nothing else than sadness of the heart."

For a king to notice and diagnose the problem wrong with a mere cup bearer was nothing but divine favor, and Nehemiah was scared by the king's concern and what the king said, "Then I was very much afraid." These were the words of Nehemiah before he answered the king and said,

"Let the king live forever! Why should not my face be sad when the city, the place of my fathers' sepulchers, lays waste, and its gates have been destroyed by fire" - (Nehemiah 2:2b-3)

Recall that when Nehemiah heard the news about the deplorable state that the Jews remaining in Jerusalem were living and that the city had been burnt by fire, he wept, fasted and committed everything to the hand of God, and that should be the attitude of every child of God when you hear a sad and discouraging news and when you are being discouraged from pursuing your set goals and objective, or when your God-given purpose is under threat. Because from that point on when you pray and commit everything into the hands of God, His divine favor and protection will follow you, and divine favor was now working for Nehemiah before the king.

In (Nehemiah 2:4-6) says,

"Then the king said to me, for what do you make request?"

But Nehemiah being a committed child and one that believed in the awesome power of God to grant him divine favor, prayed to God first before he put his request to the king.

And he said to the king,

"If it pleases the king, and if your servant has found favor in your sight, that you send me to Judah, to the city of my fathers' sepulchers that I might rebuild it." - (Nehemiah 2:5)

To the less spiritually inclined, it might look like, Nehemiah was already in the presence of the king, and the king had asked him to make his request, why not go ahead and present his request instead of first praying to God, but Nehemiah knew that the actual power to grant his request was not with the king, but power is only in the hand of the God who created heaven and earth, and even the king himself.

In (Nehemiah 2:6) says,

"And the king said to me (the queen sitting beside him) 'How long will you be gone, and when will you return?"

Now the king had not only granted Nehemiah request, but he wanted to know how long it would take to finish the work of God that Nehemiah had set himself to do. Because of the prayer that Nehemiah offered to God, and his absolute faith and belief that the God he served will grant him divine favor in the presence of the king, Nehemiah was bold enough to ask the king for more favor and all that he requested for was granted to him by the king.

In (Nehemiah 2:8b) it says,

"And the king granted me what I asked, for the good hand of my God was upon me"

With this statement from Nehemiah, you will now understand that he knew from the beginning that the king would not grant his request if God did not sanction it. So don't at any time listen to discouragement in pursuit of inspired goals because mere man that can't predict the number of his days on earth and that his breadth is in the hands of God, to dictate, influence or discourage you from pursuing your personal goals, or the purpose of God for your life.

When you have a goal, a vision or mission to accomplish, first do exactly what Nehemiah did. Go to God in prayer and fasting, and humbly ask him to give you the needed focus, direction and divine favor to accomplish all that you set out to do. Because when the hand of God is upon you, and you put him in charge of that goal or vision, then there is nothing any man can do to stop you, and no discouragement that comes your way can hinder you from fulfilling all you have in mind to do.

It is true that there is no great accomplishment that doesn't attract some level of opposition and discouragement, because people that hate you and that don't believe in your goal and vision will do everything possible to place obstacles in your path in order for you to fail and never accomplish your dream. But because God is on your side, and

His divine favor is with you, you will overcome all obstacles and discouragement and come out victorious.

That was exactly the case of Nehemiah, for even after he had obtained favor from God which made the king to grant his request, there was still opposition from people who did not share in his vision and people who felt they had nothing to benefit from the good work he wanted to do.

In (Nehemiah 2:10) it says,

"But when Sanballat the Horonite and Tobiah the servant, the Ammonite, heard this, it displeased them greatly that someone had come to seek the welfare of the children of Israel."

So if you think that everyone around you, including friends and family are happy of that your new goal, that your new vision that will propel you to enviable heights, or that work of God that will bring glory to God's kingdom and make your name known all over the world, then you have to think again. If you think that everyone is going to line up behind you and encourage you to succeed in your new goal, then you are not fully prepared for the big task ahead.

The goal is your goal and not theirs. Your vision is only clear to you, and they might even be threatened by your goal because it doesn't align with theirs and they have nothing to benefit from it, so they will rather discourage you and put obstacles in your path than encourage you. At this point, because you have committed everything you want to accomplish in the hands of God, you have nothing to fear or worry about, because the God you trust and serve will go before you to make you path straight and demolish all obstacles that is standing in your path to progress.

When Nehemiah presented his goals to the children of Israel, they keyed into his vision, but the people benefitting from the evil that had befallen Jerusalem and that didn't support his goal mocked and discouraged them.

"But when Sanballat the Horonite and Tobiah the servant, the Ammonite, and Geshem the Arab heard of it, they derided

us and despised us and said, what is this thing that you are doing? Are you rebelling against the king? Then I replied them, the God of heaven will make us prosper, and we his servants will arise and build: but you have no portion or right or memorial in Jerusalem."

But despite all the discouragement that Nehemiah was facing from the people that do not want him to succeed in the goal that he had set out to accomplish, the job went on smoothly and the remaining Jews where cooperative because the hand of God was upon it. So whatever work, task or goal you have set out to achieve, commit it to the hand of God, and once the hand of God is upon it, no discouragement or opposition will ever make you fail. The word of God says in (Proverbs 16:3),

"Commit thy works unto the Lord, and thy thoughts shall be established."

Only in God's hand will your plans, goals and purpose succeed and prosper despite the discouragement of your enemies. In (Nehemiah

4:1) it is recorded that even when the enemies of Nehemiah heard that the job of rebuilding the places that were destroyed by fire was succeeding and moving smoothly, they were very angry and filled with rage because they never expected him to succeed despite all the discouragement he has gotten from them. So they mocked and ridiculed the good job they were doing.

But these things and the wicked and evil words coming out from the mouth of the enemies of Nehemiah did not deter him, but instead he remained strong and prayed to God saying:

"Hear, O God, for we are despised, turn back their taunt upon their own heads, and give them up to be plundered in a land where they are captives. Do not cover their guilt's, and let no their sin be blotted out from thy site; for the have provoked thee to anger before the builders." - (Nehemiah 4:4-5)

Your enemies and those that really want to discourage you so that you fail will not give up easily, at least not until they see you fail, so don't react negatively or be afraid of them, but pray and commit them into the hands of God as Nehemiah did and God will handle them for you.

How To React When You Are Being Discouraged

Start by praying. It can really be overwhelming when we are being discouraged and when obstacles stand in our way to achieving our goal, but you should never let that be a reason to throw in the towel and quit from pursuing your goal and accomplishing your God-given purpose on earth.

The truth is that, no matter how discouraged you are, God cares for you and He wants to help you carry the burden. He knows how you feel right now, and how discouraged you have become, so he is waiting and ever ready for you to seek his face and ask Him for help, and He will guide you through the path to follow and the ways to accomplish your goals through the guidance of the Holy Spirit.

Pray for God to send His Spirit to strengthen you and give you the capacity to turn discouragement into a motivational stepping stone to achieve your goal. Pray for God's divine favor to be upon you, so that whatever you need to accomplish your goal will be effortlessly provided for you, and anyone or anything standing in your way of success will be removed. Praying to God in times of discouragements enables you to shift the focus from yourself and transfer your worries to someone that has the capacity to handle the discouragement you face, and because His character is consistent with helping those that call on Him in times of need, God will help you deal with discouragement.

Be prepared. Great things are achieved by great people, and they don't achieve it without facing some degree of obstacles or discouragements along the way. There is a popular saying which says,

"You can't make an omelet without breaking and egg."

So if your desire is to accomplish a great goal and fulfill a great purpose of God in your life, then you need to be strong and prepare for the challenges and discouragement that you will face.

If you take a proper look in the bible, you will discover that all the men who achieved great things and had great goals to accomplish were faced with one challenge or the other, and they encountered a lot of obstacles that will discourage them from fulfilling the task that set out to do, but because they were prepared, they were able to overcome.

Even Jesus, that was divinely ordained for His ministry was faced with discouragement even from His own family members.

So discouragement is nothing new, all you have to do is to ask God to prepare for you to be able to withstand and defeat discouragement when it comes.

Stand in faith and eliminate fear. If your assignment or goal is divinely motivated and one that is going to benefit a lot of people, especially the children of God, then you have to know that the devil through his agents will do everything possible to discourage you and make sure that you fail.

So you need to stand in faith on God's promises concerning you, and eliminate any form of fear that might discourage you and make you quit on what you want to achieve personally for yourself and what God has divinely ordained for you to accomplish.

If you become afraid that the discouragement you are getting might derail or destroy your plans to achieve your goals, don't panic, but commit it to God and have faith that He will see you through.

Lessons to learn from Nehemiah to enable you stand firm in the face of discouragement.

The life and story of Nehemiah is one that is mixed with courage, commitment, zeal and fear of the Lord, and the love he had for his people and Jerusalem, but what I found so interesting is the level of inspiration to be taken away from the way and manner that he went about the work of rebuilding Jerusalem even in the face of obstacles, discouragement and even threat to his Life.

Let us take a look at some of the inspiring lessons in Nehemiah's life to enable us learn how to face obstacles and discouragements.

Ask God to help you. When Nehemiah heard about the situation in Jerusalem, and how the place had been burnt with fire and the suffering of the Jews in that place, he did not just arise and start making personal plans on how to rebuild the burnt city of Jerusalem and help the Jews living there, but he reacted positively the way every child of God that believes in Him and trusts in His capacity to help us in times of need.

In (Nehemiah 1:4-5) it says,

"When I heard these words I sat down and wept, and mourned for days, and I continued fasting, and praying before the God of heaven. And I said 'O Lord God of Heaven, the great and terrible God who keeps covenant and steadfast love with

those who love Him and keep His commandment."

Nehemiah knew that the task ahead was far bigger than him, so the first thing he did was to ask God for help and to remind Him of his promises and covenant with the people of Israel. So if your aim is to succeed at any goal you want to undertake, and surmount any form of obstacle and discouragement that is standing in your way to achieve the desired success you desire, then you need to ask God for help before you begin in that project. When you ask God for help before you begin a project, He comes in and takes charge and when He takes charge, success is guaranteed.

Make prayer your tool. In anything you want to accomplish, and any goal you want to achieve, it is very important you start with prayer.

During the ministry of Jesus Christ, He never did anything very important without first praying to the Father for about it. Prayer is the most powerful way we talk to God, and hear His instructions and guidance on how to go about the task at hand.

Diligence In Doing The Job

We see the way Nehemiah went about doing the job diligently, how committed he was in seeing that the city of Jerusalem is rebuilt even with little resources and in the face of opposition and discouragement.

The bible says,

"Whatever your task, work heartily, as serving the Lord and not men. Knowing that from the Lord, you will receive the inheritance as your reward: you are serving the Lord Christ." - (Colossians 3:23-24)

God desires us to do all our work with diligence and with great honesty and when we meet all these criteria, God will stand firm for us to make sure that whatever task that we undertake will come out very successful despite any opposition. And it was the diligence that Nehemiah employed in doing his work in the presence of the king as if he was serving God and no man that made him to receive favor and blessing from God and the king.

Employ diligence in whatever you do, and it will distinguish you and propel you to achieve the success you desire even in the face of discouragement. The bible says in (Proverbs 22:29),

"Seest thou a man diligent in his business? He shall stand before kings; he shall not stand before mere men."

Be strong and focused on the goal you want to achieve. In the face of opposition and discouragement, it is very easy for the weak and faint hearted to give up and quit on the goal they have planned to achieve, but that was not the case with Nehemiah, and because he had prayed and asked God for help, he was resolute and strong in the face of discouragement and opposition.

And that attitude of strength and perseverance is something we must employ when doing any meaningful task in our life, because it is very easy to make plans and start a project, but it not easy to follow through and finish the project when we face discouraging situations.

Nehemiah was strong, focused and motivated, and he was able to muster the support of others because they saw these qualities in him. In (Nehemiah 2:17-18) it reads,

"Then I said to them, you see the trouble we are in, how Jerusalem lies in ruins with its gates burned. Come let us build the wall of Jerusalem, that we may no longer suffer disgrace. And I told them about the hand of my God which has been upon me for good and also the words which the king has spoken to me. And they said, let us rise up and build. So they strengthened their hands for the work."

When you exhibit these positive attitude of strength, focus, direction and perseverance, people will key into your goal and work with you to succeed and your enemies and discouragers will fade away because they know that you mean business, but even when they try, they will fail woefully just like the enemies of Nehemiah.

It is only through faith that we can achieve. God is a good and caring God, and he is ever ready and willing to support, guide and lead us through the right path to follow in achieving our desired goals.

So we need to have absolute faith that God is willing and able to help us to navigate and face the discouragement and opposition that we face in our way to success and come out victorious and successful. Nehemiah trusted God, and exhibited unshakable faith in the ability of God to help and deliver His people in times of need. So despite the danger, opposition, threat of life that he faced, he maintain faith and trust in God.

Don't give room for you opponents and discouragers to get to you. When you are resolute and passionate about achieving your goals and the hand of God is upon you in every step that you take, the enemy and opposition will realize that they have no power to stop you from not realizing your goal.

At this point, your discouragers might come with a subtle move to negotiate with you, or pretend that they don't really hate you, but it is all a lie and a ploy and a way to take advantage of you and destroy you.

In the case of Nehemiah, when his enemies and discouragers saw that the work was progressing effectively despite all they have done to stop it, they changed tactics and pretended to try and negotiate with Nehemiah. In (Nehemiah 6:2-4) it says,

"Sanballat and Gershom sent to me, saying Come and let us meet together in one of the villages in the plain of Ono', but they intended to do me harm. And I sent messages to them saying I am doing a great work and I can't come down. Why should the work stop while I leave it and come down to you. And they sent to me four times in this way, and I answered them in the same manner."

So Nehemiah was able to use wisdom and the divine favor and help from God to rebuilt the walls of Jerusalem and restore glory to Jerusalem despite the opposition and discouragement that came his way.

Prayer Points

Father, your word says in (Isaiah 54:17) that,

"No weapon formed against you shall prosper, and any tongue which rises against you in judgment shall be condemned."

So I pray today that any plan or weapon of the enemy to put obstacle or discourage me from pursuing my goals in life will backfire on their head in Jesus name. Amen.

Father, your words said in (Proverbs 16:3),

"Commit thy works unto the Lord, and thy thoughts shall be established."

So Father, in the name of your Son Jesus Christ, I commit all my goals and the works of my hands into your able hands, believing that no obstacle and discouragement that comes my way shall stop me from achieving success and prospering in Jesus name. Amen.

Father, give me the wisdom and grace to start all my endeavors and task with prayer and fasting because only through prayer and fasting can the obstacles in my way be demolished and all my encouragers defeated, just as it is written in (Nehemiah 1:4) which says,

"When I heard these words I sat down and wept, and mourned for days; and I continued fasting and praying before the God of heaven."

Thank you Father, in Jesus name, Amen.

In (Nehemiah 2:8b) the bible says,

> ***"And the king granted me what I asked, for the good hand of my God was upon me"***

Father, I pray for the grace to receive divine favor from you and from men, so that whatever task or pursuit I put my hand to achieve will prosper despite any evil discouragement in Jesus name. Amen.

In (Nehemiah 2:10) it says,

> ***"But when Sanballat the Horonite and Tobiah the servant, the Ammonite, heard this, it displeased them greatly that***

someone had come to seek the welfare of the children of Israel."

Father, today by the fire of the Holy Ghost, I decree that any unfriendly friend, colleague, or enemy that is displeased by my progress in life and the goal in my life shall be consumed by fire in Jesus name. Amen.

Father, your word says in (Colossians 3:23-24) that,

"Whatever your task, work heartily, as serving the Lord and not men. Knowing that from the Lord, you will receive the inheritance as your reward: you are serving the Lord Christ."

So Father, in the name of your Son Jesus, I ask for the zeal and motivation to do my work heartily in order to get my reward from you and not from men in Jesus name. Amen.

It is written in (Proverbs 22:29),

"Seest thou a man diligent in his business? He shall stand before kings; he shall not stand before mere men."

My God, the creator of heaven and earth, the giver of all good things, I pray for strength and diligence to pursue my goals, to excel and achieve success and to triumph over any form of discouragement.

Father, your word says in (Philippians 4:13) that,

"I can do all things through Christ who strengthens me."

Father, thank you because you are always there for me, thank you because through your Son Jesus Christ you have already given me the strength and capability to do all things. Thank you because every obstacle and discouragement has been trampled under my foot in Jesus name. Amen.

It is written,

"And we know that for those who love God all things work together for good, for

those who are called according to his purpose." - (Roman 8:28)

So in the name of Jesus, I decree that every obstacle, every discouragement that comes my way in the pursuit of my goals and purpose in life shall turn to my good and progress in the mighty name of Jesus. Amen.

Chapter 4: Why Does God Allow Adversities In Our Lives?

God sometimes allows us to face trials, adversities, afflictions and tribulations so that we can learn some very important lessons in our lives. These experiences refine, define and shape our mindset into understanding the workings of God and how far reaching is His love and mercy towards us. Adversity still helps us to view the world and everything around us from a different perspective in order to change our behavior for the better. Our heavenly Father knows all that is good and profitable to us, so whenever we are facing trials and adversity, we should look for the lessons to be learnt from it.

First, we need to see adversity from a positive perspective and appreciate why God sometimes allows it to happen. James, one of Apostles of Jesus Christ, puts it in a way that helps us understand the purpose of adversity and its far reaching benefits when he wrote,

> ***"Brethren, count it all joy when ye fall into diverse temptation; knowing this, that the trying of your faith worketh patience. But let patience have her perfect work, that ye may be perfect and entire wanting nothing" - (James 1:2-4).***

With this verse of the bible, you will see that God does not allow adversity simply to punish us and make us suffer for sins committed, but to refine us, to teach us to be patient, create a perfect work in our life and strengthen us to lack nothing.

Apostle Paul, who should know better because he suffered series of trials and temptations, faced a lot of adversity throughout his ministry on earth for the uplifting and glorifying of the name of Jesus. Paul puts it this way,

> ***"More than that, we rejoice in our sufferings, knowing that suffering produces endurance, and endurance produces character, and character produces hope, and hope does not disappoint us, because God's love has been poured into our hearts through the***

Holy Spirit which he has given to us." - (Romans 5:3-5)

Adversity, trials and temptations should not be seen as a way God makes us suffer, but as means to direct, refocus and align our attention to His purpose for our lives. God uses adversity to accomplish His divine mandate in us, because it is written in (Romans 8:28-29)

"We know that in everything God works for good for those who love him, who are called according to His purpose. For those whom He foreknew He also predestined to be conformed to the image of His Son, in order that He might be the first born among many brethren."

So, God wants us to have an image like that of His Son, an image that is pure and well refined, and for God to have those who are pure like the image of His son, He purifies and refines them. And sometimes God does that by allowing adversity in our lives. There are those that God has called for His purpose and glory, and just like the only begotten Son of God went through trials, temptations and adversity in order to accomplish the purpose for which God sent him to earth, so shall the ones chosen and called by God face one form of adversity to accomplish God's will on earth. "And those whom He predestined, He also called; and those whom He called, He also justified; and those whom He justified He also glorified.

God allows adversity for the following reasons:

Our Attention Is Focused On God In Times Of Adversity

In times of trials, temptations and adversity, our focus and attention is on God.

Adversity makes us to realize that it is time to stop relying on our own strength, our own wisdom and understanding, but to rely on God's given wisdom and understanding in solving our problems. Adversity makes us to refocus our priorities, and seek the face of God in the task, goals and plans we have for our lives, to know if it is God's will to pursue those our heart desires. The truth is that, humans are used to pursuing personal ambitions without seeking the face of God in whatever they want to do, but in times of trials and adversity, we pause for a while, to know what God wants, and ask for His wisdom and help in accomplishing the tasks, goals and plans we have for our lives.

Adversity and trials bring out the weakness in us, and when we are weak and all hope in our personal strength, wisdom and understanding is lost and our own strength has failed us, we go back to God relying on his strength to deliver us from all forms of problems that we are facing.

One of the major purposes of adversity is to reposition us to desire more of Jesus Christ in our life and to appreciate what He did for us on the cross of Calvary. Adversity shows that on our own can't do anything, but we can do much and achieve much more through Christ who is our strength.

Jesus knew we would face trials and adversity, and that we would need the help of God in those times, hence He said in (Mathew 11:28-30).

"Come unto me, all ye that labor and are heavy laden, and I will give you rest. Take my yoke upon you, and learn of me; for I am meek and lowly in heart; and ye shall find rest unto your souls, for my yoke is easy and my burden is light."

Apostle Paul endured and suffered a lot of adversity willingly and happily in order to draw closer to Christ and partake in the resurrection power of Jesus Christ. In (Philippians 3:8-9), he wrote,

"Indeed I count everything as loss because of the surpassing worth of knowing Christ Jesus my Lord. For His sake I have suffered the loss of all things, and count them as refuse, in order that I may gain Christ, and be found in Him not having a righteousness of my own, based on law, but that which is through faith, Christ the righteousness from God that depends on faith."

So, in order to get the best out of trial and adversity, we should have a positive mind about it and see it as means that God uses to get our attention because He wants us to rely on Him. He wants to strengthen us, refine us, purify us and give us the patience to live a peaceful and successful life.

Adversity Proves That God Loves Us

In times of adversity, the love of God manifests more when we completely trust Him and commit the situation into His able care.

There is no good and caring father that will want his child to go astray and perish in the process, but they will instead discipline that child in order to refine, reform and bring out the very best in that child. This is exactly the way our heavenly Father operates, because He loves and cares for us and doesn't want us to perish, He allows trials and adversity in our lives in order to get the best out of us.

God disciplines His children and all those that He loves in order to make them mature, disciplined and steadfast in His ways. God is a very loving and caring father and He uses adversity to make us learn and become even more like He is.

In (Hebrews 12:5-9) it says,

> ***"My son, does not regard lightly the discipline of the Lord, nor lose courage when you are punished by Him. For the Lord discipline him whom he loves and chastises every son whom he receives. It is for discipline that you have to endure. God is treating you as sons; for what son is there whom the father does not discipline? If you are left without discipline, in which all have participated, then you are illegitimate children not sons."***

This is telling us how God values and loves us as His own children, how He has taken us as His legitimate children, the heirs with Christ to the kingdom. If we are co-heirs with Christ indeed, God ought to discipline us when we fall out of line in order for us not to miss out on the glorious inheritance He has prepared for us, and adversity and trials are some of the ways that God allows to keep us in check.

God's discipline might look painful and too much to bear for us, but if we trust in Him and persevere, it will be to our own benefit, and yield positive fruits that will refine, remold and bring out the very best out of us. So, if the trial and adversity is making you feel tired and weighed down, you need to change your attitude right away and see it that God is working for your own good, because in (Hebrews 12:12) the bible says

"Therefore lift your dropping hands and strengthen your weak knees, and make straight paths for your feet, so that what is lame may not be put out of joint but rather be healed."

Change your mindset and see the hand of God in any situation that seems to overwhelm you, because that situation might be the stepping stone that God has placed in your path to elevate you to that enviable height that you have always dreamed of.

Adversity Makes Us More Accountable To God

The bible tells us in (Proverbs 9:10) that,

"The fear of the Lord is the beginning of wisdom."

But if you are not accountable to God, or God is not holding you accountable to all your deeds on earth, then how can you fear Him?

It is in the period of trial and adversity that we subject ourselves to God's will and become accountable to Him, and it is in those periods that we value and acknowledge the presence of God more in our lives. A lot of us tend to forget that there is a God that rules in the affairs of men, God that created heaven and earth and everything that is in it, so we begin to live our lives as if we own it, and as if we have the capacity to determine or change our destinies.

It is at this point and this type of attitude that makes God to remind us who is in charge and who created us in the first place, so He removes His protection and allows adversity to come in order to remind us that He is God and all accountability should be to Him only. God did this in the life of the children of Israel to remind them that He is God and for them to turn from their evil ways and become accountable to Him.

In (Judges 2:20-22), the bible says,

"So the anger of the Lord was kindled against Israel; and he said because this people have transgressed my covenant which I commanded their fathers, and have not obeyed my voice. I will no longer drive out before them any of the nations that Joshua left when he died, that by them I may test Israel, whether they will take care to walk in the way of the Lord as their fathers did, or not."

This verse shows that when you forget who God is to you, and disregard all His benefits toward, in the sense that you start living a life of sin and iniquity, God can in His anger, allow adversity to come into your life in order to bring your attention back to Him.

Adversity Makes Us Hate Sin And Draw Close To God

The word of God says that sin is a reproach, but that righteousness exalts a nation.

Sin is one of the main reasons adversity comes into our life and the pain and trouble that adversity brings makes us to know the futility of sin and hate it. Then when we have recognized the negative effect of sin in our life and the adversity that it attracts into our lives, it makes us draw closer to God and commit our lives into His hand.

God employs discipline to help His children to live the type of life that He intends them to live, so when we are under trial and adversity, it is the ideal time to re-examine how we are living our lives to know if it pleases God and if sin has taken over our life. In (Revelations 3:19) it says,

> ***"As many as I love, I rebuke and chasten; be zealous therefore, and repent."***

This was a warning to the church in Laodicea when they were going astray and living contrary to the will of God.

God uses adversity to make His beloved children dead to sin and its influence in their lives, and to become more alive in Jesus and able to obtain the power of the Spirit of God rather than walking in the flesh. So, we should use God's word as a beacon and point of reference to examine our lives and see where we are going against the will of God and repent immediately in order not to attract adversity into our life.

There are some warnings in the bible that show us the consequences of sin and how it can bring reproach and adversity into our life.

"He who conceals his transgressions will not prosper, but he who confesses and forsakes them will obtain mercy - (Proverbs 28:13).

"Blessed is the man who fears the Lord always, but he who hardens his heart will fall into calamity." - (Proverb 28:14)

"If a man returns evil for good, evil will not depart from his house" - (Proverbs 17:13).

"For the wages of sin is death, but the free gift of God is eternal life in Christ Jesus our Lord." - (Romans 6:23)

"There is a way that seems right to a man, but its end is the way to death." - (Proverbs 14:12)

Adversity Is A Proof Of Spiritual Battle

Adversity in our life is a proof that there is a spiritual warfare going, and as children of the Most High God, we should always be alert and know that there is constant warfare between God fighting on our behalf and the forces of darkness that want to undermine the move of God in our life.

These adversities come in the form of crisis and trouble in our life and family, sickness, weariness and oppressions of all kinds, but when these adversities come, stand firm and have faith in God, because with Him victory is guaranteed.

(Ephesians 6:11-13) tells us what to do and how to react in such situations, it says,

"Put on the whole armor of God that you may stand against the wiles of the devil, for we are not contending against flesh and blood, but against the principalities, against the powers, against the rulers of this present darkness, against the spiritual host of wickedness in the heavenly places. Therefore take the whole armor of God that you may be able to withstand in the evil day, and having done all to stand."

And for you to be able to stand firm and withstand the warfare and attacks of the evil one in times of adversity, you need to possess some godly virtues and qualities, or else you will be found wanting and exposed to the enemy. Such virtues like truth, righteousness, peace and faith.

"Stand therefore, having girded your loins with truth, and having put on the breastplate of righteousness, and having shod your feet with the equipment of the gospel of peace, besides all these, taking the shield of faith, with which you can you

can quench all the flaming darts of the evil one. And take the helmet of salvation, and the world of the spirit, which is the word of God." - (Ephesians 6:14-17)

At this point of warfare and adversity, when the evil one is throwing evil darts at you to cause trouble and crisis in your life, you need to make praying in the spirit at all times one of your biggest and most effective weapon, because constant and consistent prayer keeps your spirit alert to overcome the devices of the enemy.

Adversity Destroys The Pride In Us

God hates pride, and He can't tolerate or work with someone that is proud, and pride is one of the sins that attract adversity and trials into people's life.

And God allows adversity into the life of someone that is proud in order to humble them and make them focus their attention on God and not in themselves and in their own knowledge and understanding. In (James 4:6-8) says

"But He gives more grace; therefore it says 'God opposes the proud, but gives grace to the humble.' Submit yourselves therefore to God. Resist the devil and He will flee from you. Draw near to God and He will draw near to you, cleanse your hands, and purify your hearts, you men of double mind."

Adversity exposes the level of pride in our lives, and makes us to know that we don't have the answers and solutions to our problems, so we humble ourselves and submit ourselves to God. Thus, when you are facing trials and adversity, reexamine your life to see if you have pride in you, and if you notice that there have been areas in your life where pride is taking the place of God, then you need as a matter of urgency to confess your sin of pride, humble yourself before God, and pray for His grace to overcome pride and come out of adversity.

These Bible verses show that God hates pride and that pride can bring adversity into our lives.

"When pride comes, then comes disgrace, but with humble is wisdom." - (Proverbs 11:2)

"By insolence the heedless makes strife, but with those who take advice is wisdom." - (Proverbs 13:10)

"A man's pride will bring him low, by he who is lowly in spirit will obtain honor." - (Proverbs 29:23)

"For everyone who exalts himself will be humbled, and he who humbles himself will be exalted." - (Luke 14:11)

"The fear of the Lord is hatred of evil. Pride and arrogance and the way of evil and perverted speech I hate." - (Proverbs 8:13)

"Everyone who is arrogant in heart is an abomination to the Lord; be assured, he will not go unpunished." - (Proverbs 16:15)

"For all that is in the world, the desires of the flesh and the desires of the eyes and pride in possession, is not from the Father but is from the world." - (1 John 2:16)

"Pride comes before destruction and a haughty spirit before a fall." - (Proverbs 16:18)

"Live in harmony with one another. Do not be haughty, but associate with the lowly. Never be wise in your own sight." - (Romans 12:16)

"The haughty looks of man shall be brought low, and the lofty pride of man shall be humbled, and the Lord alone will be exalted in that day." - (Isaiah 2:11)

Adversity Teaches Us Empathy And Love For Others

For anyone that has gone through the pain of trial and adversity, it is very easy to understand what others are going through and show empathy by encouraging and comforting them.

As adversity helps us receive God's comfort, and we are then able to show love and comfort to other people who are going through what we went through.

In (2 Corinthians 1:3) it says,

> **"Blessed be the God and Father of our Lord Jesus Christ, the Father of mercies and God of all comfort. Who comforts us in our affliction, so that we may be able to comfort those who are in any affliction, with the comfort with which we ourselves are comforted by God? For as we share abundantly in Christ sufferings, so through Christ we share abundantly in comfort too."**

So if you are selfish and don't have love to share with others, God can allow adversity in your life in order for you to learn how to love and comfort others when He Himself has loved and comforted you in times of adversity.

God Uses Adversity To Glorify His Name

God is the source of all good things and all good and precious gifts come from Him. God's glory brings joy and salvation and everything God does for His glory is for our own benefit and edification.

So when adversity comes into your life, don't despair or give up hope, but commit it to God and He will glorify His great and holy name by having mercy on you and delivering you from every trial and affliction you are passing through.

(Isaiah 48:10-11) says,

> *"Behold, I have refined you, but not like silver; I have tried you in the furnace of affliction. For my own sake, for my own sake I do it, for how should my name be profaned? My glory I will not give to another."*

As children of God, we need to know that everything on earth was made by God and for His own glory. And whatever exalts the name of God works to bring out the best in us.

The disciples of Jesus Christ once asked what sin the man who was born blind commit to warrant his condition, to which He answered them saying,

"It was not that this man sinned, or his parents, but that the works of God might be made manifest in him." - (John 9:3)

God is God of love and mercy, and He is not looking around for who to afflict, but when adversity comes into our life through the evil one, God can use it to bring glory to His name to make us know that the ultimate power of healing and deliverance lies with Him.

God Uses Adversity To Confirm Us As Sons And Co-Heirs With Christ

As Christians and children of God, going through trials and experiencing adversity for the advancement of God's kingdom is part of the heritage that we have in God, because God uses it to test our faithfulness and to strengthen us to be able to do the work that He has assigned us to do.

When you look through the bible, and check the lives of men that God used to do exploit and bring glory to His name, you will notice that they all at one time or the other passed through trials, tribulations, persecution and other forms of adversity. If you check the life of Apostle Paul, you will see that he suffered different forms of adversity such as beatings, imprisonment, shipwrecks, bitten by deadly poisonous snake, mockery and personal affliction, but he endured all because of the glory of God.

All the disciples of Jesus suffered adversity and they died as martyrs because of the faith they had in Christ Jesus. The truth is that as Christians, we will go through adversity, and there was never any time that God or His only begotten Son Jesus Christ said that everything is going to be rosy and sweet, but that we are going to face adversity and His grace will be sufficient for us to overcome and come out victorious.

Christ told us in (John 16:33),

"I have said this to you, that in me you may have peace. In the world you have

tribulation, but be of good cheer, I have overcome the world."

The word of God in the bible admonishes us not to put all our focus on what we have on this earth and the life we are living on this earth, but to work diligently to make heaven, because whatever form of trial, tribulation and adversity that we are facing on earth right now as children of God can't be compared to the glory that God has already prepared for us in heaven.

As children of God, if we are not ready and willing to share in the sufferings and discipline that God uses to confirm us as sons and co-heirs with Christ, then we will not be partakers of His heavenly glory. (Romans 8:16-18) says,

"It is the spirit himself bearing witness with our spirit that we are children of God. And if children then heirs, heirs of God and fellows with Christ, provided we suffer in Him in order that we may also be glorified with Him. I consider that the sufferings of this present time are not

worth comparing with the glory that is to be revealed to us."

Learn to endure trials and adversity and any form of discipline that God uses to refine and strengthen you because God loves you and He takes you as a son or daughter, for which father will not discipline a son or daughter that he loves. And you have forgotten the word of encouragement that addresses you as sons:

"My son do not make light of the Lord's discipline, and do not lose heart when He rebukes you, because the Lord disciplines those He loves, and he punishes everyone he accepts as a son."

In (Proverbs 3:11-12) it says,

"My son, do not despise the Lord's discipline or be weary of His reproof, for the Lord reproves him whom He loves, as a father the son in whom he delights."

God used adversity to mold Apostle Paul into a disciple that did great exploits to advance the kingdom of God and preach the name of Christ.

In fact adversity so strengthened Apostle Paul that he became the greatest apostle of Christ and wrote a lot of books in the New Testament.

Paul knew that all the suffering he was going through and the adversity that he faced at every point of preaching the gospel of Christ was for his own good and not a form of punishment from God for the sins he committed, so he maintained a positive perspective throughout all his trials and tribulations.

And Paul had this to say in (2 Corinthians 4:7-11).

> ***"But we have this treasure in earthen vessels, to show that the transcendent power belongs to God and not us. We are afflicted in every way, but not crushed, perplexed, but not driven to despair, persecuted, but not forsaken, struck down, but not destroyed; always carrying in the body the death of Jesus, so that the life of Jesus may be manifest in our bodies, for while we live we are always given up to death for Jesus' sake, so that***

the life of Jesus may be manifest in our mortal flesh."

Apostle Paul fully understands the working of God, and the reasons why He sometimes allow adversity into the lives of His beloved children, so that is why instead of being weakened by the myriads of afflictions, trials, persecutions, physical health problems that he went through, he became strengthened and motivated by it and achieved far more than any of the other disciples of Jesus.

So stop seeing the trials and adversity in your life as punishment and as a sign that God doesn't love you, but as a sign that He is bringing out the best in you because He loves you. In (Romans 5:3-5), it is written

"More than that, we rejoice in our sufferings, knowing that sufferings produce endurance and endurance produces character, and character produces hope, and hope doesn't disappoint us, because God's love has

been poured into our hearts through the Holy Spirit which has been given to us."

Some Basic Things To Know In Times Of Adversity

In times of trial and adversity, the first thing that we have to understand in order to be patient and react positively is that God is a loving and caring Father, and that He has a purpose why He allow adversity to come into our lives.

God is aware of everything that happens to his children, so care must be taken in order not to lose the vital lessons that God wants us to learn in that period, and to miss the opportunity that He wants to use to build and refine us. (Romans 8:28-29) says,

"We know that in everything God works for good with those who love him, who are called according to His purpose. For those whom he foreknew he also predestined to conform to the image of His son, in order that he might be the first-born among many brethren."

In (Roman 8:28), the bible makes us to understand the reality of life as believers, in the sense that not all of our experience in life is going to be rosy and sweet, but that anything that happens to the child of God will work for good. So with this understanding of how God works, we need not to despair or lose hope in times of adversity, but to prayerfully ask him to show us the purpose of the adversity.

Secondly, we should know that much grace abound in times of adversity, and that God in his infinite mercy, will provide abundant grace, mercy and the strength that we need to face adversity and come out victorious

Don't lose faith on God's promises no matter how hard that situation looks. (1 Corinthians 10:13) says,

"No temptation has overtaken you that is not common to man. God is faithful, and He will not let you be tempted beyond your strength, but with the temptation will He also provide the way of escape, that you may be able to endure it."

(Hebrews 4:15-16) still tells us how God will stand for us and rescue us in times of need when it said,

"For we have not a high priest who is unable to sympathize with our weaknesses, but one who in every respect has been tempted as we are, yet without sin. Let us then with confidence draw near to the throne of grace, that we may receive mercy and find grace to help in time of need."

We need to know and understand that the only way we can face trials and adversity and come out victorious, is to hand everything to God. Let Him take total control and let His will be done.

When David was going through trials and tribulations, he didn't rely on his own strength even as a king with the whole army of Israel at his disposal, but he relied totally on God and committed his problems unto his able care. In (Psalm 23:4), God says,

"Even though I walk through the valley of the shadow of death, I fear no evil; for

thou art with me; thy rod and thy staff, they comfort me."

God is your source of strength and comfort in times of need. Go to Him humbly in prayer and fasting and he will deliver you.

Prayer Points

Father, I thank and exalt your Holy name, I thank you for you are the all-knowing God, and I thank you because you know my situation and why I am going through it. Father let your word in (Romans 5:3-4) which says,

"More than that, we rejoice in our sufferings, knowing that suffering produces endurance, and endurance produces character, and character produces hope."

Find fulfillment in my life in Jesus name, Amen.

Father, your word says in (Mathew 11:28),

"Come unto me, all ye that labor and are heavy laden, and I will give you rest."

So Father, I humbly come today unto your throne of glory asking you to please take the burden of pain, sickness and poverty out of my life and give me rest, healing and prosperity in Jesus name. Amen.

Father, your word says in (Hebrews 12:5-6),

"My son, do not regard lightly the discipline of the Lord, nor loose courage when you are punished by Him. For the Lord disciplines him whom he loves and chastises every son whom he receives."

So Father, I pray for the grace to go through challenges and adversity in life, knowing that you love me and truly wants the best for me in Jesus name. Amen.

Father your word says that,

"Sin is a reproach, but that righteousness exalts a nation." - (Proverbs 14:34)

Father, I plead with you today, to forgive me any sin in my life that is bringing adversity and reproach in my life and set me free in Jesus name. Amen.

It is written,

"Blessed is the man who fears the Lord always, but he who hardens his heart will fall into calamity?" - (Proverb 28:14)

Father, let the fear of your word and commandment not depart from me so that I will not become a victim of adversity and calamity in Jesus name. Amen.

Father, In (James 4:6) your word says,

"But He gives more grace; therefore it says 'God opposes the proud, but gives grace to the humble."

Father, I pray in total humility for you to forgive any form of pride and arrogance in my life that is making you far from me and bringing adversity in my life and give me the grace to humble myself before you in Jesus name. Amen.

It is written In (2 Corinthians 1:3-4) that,

"Blessed be the God and Father of our Lord Jesus Christ, the Father of mercies and God of all comfort. Who comforts us in our affliction, so that we may be able to comfort those who are in any affliction, with the comfort with which we ourselves are comforted by God?"

Father, I thank you for the comfort and restoration that you gave me in times of adversity, please give me the grace to be a source of comfort to others in need and adversity in Jesus name. Amen.

Father, in (Isaiah 48:10-11) your word says,

"Behold, I have refined you, but not like silver; I have tried you in the furnace of affliction. For my own sake, for my own sake I do it, for how should my name be profaned? My glory I will not give to another."

Father, I fall on my knees and plead for forgiveness for all the times I didn't give you glory for all the marvelous things you have done and still doing in my life. Forgive me Father, and remove any affliction in my life in Jesus name I pray. Amen.

Father, In (Psalm 23:4) your word says,

"Even though I walk through the valley of the shadow of death, I fear no evil; for thou art with me; thy rod and thy staff, they comfort me."

Father, I thank you for your love, your rod and your staff is my source of comfort and restoration in times of adversity so I have nothing to fear. I received my comfort, healing and restoration in Jesus name. Amen.

Chapter 5: How To Know That You Are Battling With Spiritual Warfare And Ways To Deal With It

The world we live in is controlled by the forces of good and evil, and we are constantly in battle with the forces of evil. These forces are unseen forces, so we are not capable of seeing them, but we should not make the mistake of thinking that they are not there or even relaxing and forgetting about them. The bible makes us to understand that,

"Our adversary the devil is roaring about looking for whom to devour."

So we should be prepared and alert in order not to become a victim.

The devil and his agents desires nothing more than to see the children of God suffer, so they manipulate and set up all forms of evil obstacles and arrows to afflict us. If you are a strong and dedicated believer with a strong zeal for the things of God, then you are a ready-made target of the devil. Because of the evil nature of the world that we are living, we can't completely run away from the attacks and warfare that the evil ones will bring our way, but we can defeat them and come out victorious every time.

God has already given us victory through the blood and name of Jesus when the bible says,

"Therefore, God has highly exalted him and bestowed on him the name which is above every name, that at the name of Jesus every knee should bow, in heaven and on earth and under the earth, and every tongue confess that Jesus Christ is Lord, to the glory of God the Father." - (Philippians 2:9-11)

So no matter how strong the warfare is and the pattern of warfare that the enemy brings, we have a weapon in the name of Jesus to fight the warfare that comes our way and obtain victory. Sometimes the children of God still fall victim to the devices and warfare of the enemy because they are not fully equipped or prepared for the warfare when it comes.

We should know that the evil forces of the enemy will not give us notice, or wait for us to be ready and fully ready before they strike us. So we should at all times be ready with prayer and the word of God as our weapon to counter the attack of the enemy. The bible has forewarned us about the ruthless and deadly nature of the enemy we are contending with when it says,

> *"For we are not contending against flesh and blood, but against the principalities, against the powers, against the world rulers of this present darkness, against the spiritual host of wickedness in the heavenly places." - (Ephesians 6:12)*

Ways To Know That We Are Under Spiritual Warfare

- **Sudden Attack And Crisis**

  This form of spiritual attack seems to come from the blue. One moment everything is sweet and rosy, and the next moment you are battling with monumental losses, battling with sickness from nowhere, you start experiencing sudden loss and problems from nowhere.

Sometimes the attacks come so fast that you that you are dazed confused and disillusioned. Like what happened in the life of Job, for the sudden attack was so fast and ruthless, that Job was totally confused and helpless about the whole thing. The sudden attacks can come in the form of unfavorable condition and sudden hatred from people who use to love you and favor you. One moment all is going well for you, and you get favor everywhere you go, and the next moment, people start to despise and manage to tolerate you. They just start hating you for no just cause. When this type of thing happens, know that you are under spiritual warfare, and the enemy has sowed seed of discord and hatred into your life.

The bible says that,

"He who digs a pit will fall into it, and a stone will come back upon him who starts it rolling." - (Proverbs 26:27)

This shall be the inheritance of all your enemies that tries to sow evil seeds of disfavor and hatred into your life in Jesus name. Amen.

But the good thing is that God will never allow the devil to totally take control of our lives or destroy us as long as we are living according to precept and principles. It is written,

"Yea, by thee I can crush a troop; and by my God I can leap over a wall. This God, his way is perfect; the promise of the Lord proves true; he is a shield for all those who take refuge in him." - (Psalms 18:29-30)

The spiritual warfare will come, the battles and attacks of the enemy will come in all forms and patterns, but the power of the

Most High God is there to protect and deliver us. In (Psalm 27:1-3) the bible says,

"The Lord is my light and my salvation; whom shall I fear? The Lord is the stronghold of my life; of whom shall I be afraid of? When evil doers assail me, uttering slanders against me, my adversaries and my foes, they shall stumble and fall. Though a host encamp against me, my heart shall no fear; though war arise against me, yet I will be confident."

- **Sudden Attack Sickness**

The devil so hates the children of God that he will do everything within his power to stop them from worshipping God in good health and happiness, and he will do anything from making them not to achieve the purpose of God for their lives.

The devil knows that a sick person can't serve God properly, or function fully in the activities that propel and uplift the word of God. The truth is that, a man that is ravaged by sickness, and that has been in the hospital for long battling from one sickness to another or a person that is looking for money to meet up with doctor's appointment, or money to treat a sick husband, wife, child or close relative can't function optimally in the propagation of the gospel, and the devil knows this, so he employs the tool of sickness during warfare to derail, discourage and destroy the children of God.

Yes, even in sickness, a committed child of God will still love God and keep his status, but in (Mathew 28:18-20) the bible says,

"And Jesus came and said to them 'all authority in heaven and on earth has been given to me. Go therefore and make disciples of all nations, baptizing them In the name of the Father and of the Son and of the Holy Spirit, teaching them to

observe all that I have commanded you, and lo I am with you always, to the close of the age."

This is the last mandate that Jesus gave His disciples before He ascended into heaven, and this mandate is one of the core foundations of the Christian faith, because every child of God, and any believer in our Lord Jesus Christ, has the mandate to win souls for the kingdom and help in spreading the good news of the gospel.

So the devil targets your health and renders you incapacitated in order for you not to fulfill this divine mandate. In (John 10:10) the bible says,

"The thief comes only to steal and kill and destroy; I came that they may have life, and have it abundantly."

The devil's main aim is to steal our joy, destroy our happiness and kill any relationship that we have with God. He knows that every true believer enjoys the love of God, and the hope of resurrection through Christ, something that he is not entitled to, so at all times, he initiates spiritual warfare with the children of God.

So no matter the types of affliction that the devil has afflicted you with in order to delay, or even deny you from participating in the divine mandate of Christ, be relaxed, and remain assured that your heavenly Father is still the one in control, only He holds the key to your life, so at the appointed time He will silence and destroy the move of the devil in your life and restore you back to your rightful place.

- **Pushed Into Temptation And Sin**

The life that we live today is characterized with struggle, and in the midst of those daily struggles is the lure of temptations and sin. So as children of God, we need to be very alert and vigilant of the devices and manipulations of the devil, because immediately we fall prey to those sins and temptations, we will open room for the devil to come in and attack us.

The devil unleashes spiritual warfare on the children of God by pushing them into sins and temptations of sexual immorality, financial misappropriation, gossip, malice and politics in the church which results into factions and break up. This type of spiritual warfare can happen to any believer, but the people that are the main target of this type of attack are church leaders and pastors. The devil will do anything within his power to disgrace them and pull them down. He wants to see scandals like sexual and financial scandal destroy the church, and negative news headlines being printed and circulated against the church and pastors.

He desires for the church to be in disunity, and believers to be humiliated, he wants Christian families to scatter and infighting among the brethren and church workers. So the children of God need to be strong in faith and prayer, and maintain spiritually alertness in order not to give room or fail victim of the devil's plan.

- ## Feeling Of Hopelessness And Suicidal Tendency

A lot of people are going through struggles in life. Things are not going the way they plan, but God sees our struggles and He intends to intervene and change our situation for the better, but the devil who is happy about your struggle, will now arise at the point that your success is about to break forth, and start filling your head with words of hopelessness and despair.

The devil will make you feel that your life is over, and that you have no hope or chance of ever making it again and that there is nothing in life worth living for. The truth is that, most anxiety, fear, depression, feeling of hopelessness, suicidal tendencies, mood swings and disorder, mental and psychological problems that a lot of people are going through, and that has made a lot of people to feel that their lives are not worth living and commit suicide is manipulation and spiritual attack by the devil and his evil agents.

The devil is mean, cruel and ruthless, and there is nothing that gives him more pleasure than seeing lives destroyed and destinies wasted. The only hope and redemption that we have from this form of manipulation and spiritual attack from the devil is to completely put our lives and trust on God and rely only on His promises.

- **A Feeling Of Guilt And Shame**

The devil can wage an emotional warfare on you, by making you feel guilty and ashamed of your past and all the wrong things you had ever done in life. He makes you so guilty and ashamed to the point where you start feeling worthless and unqualified for God's love and redemption.

This type of emotional warfare and blackmail happens slowly, but consistently and if you are not spiritually alert and prayerful, the devil will succeed in deceiving you that God doesn't want someone as dirty and bad like you, thereby separating you from God and the benefits that come from being a child of God. The bible tells us that the devil is a liar, so don't believe him when he says you are a worthless sinner before God, because it is sinners like you that made God to send His only begotten son to come into this world to save.

In (Luke 5:3), Jesus said,

"Those who are well have no need of a physician, but those who are sick. I have not come to call the righteous, but sinners to repentance."

So you see that you are not worthless in the sight of God, because of you are, God will not make His Son to come for your sake. In fact, you are so important and useful to God that He specially and specifically chose you for His redemption.

There is no sin, or crime that you have committed that will make you irredeemable in the sight of God, so don't let the devil and his evil agents make you think or believe otherwise. (Romans 3:23-25) says,

"For all have sinned and fall short of the glory of God, they are justified by his grace as a gift, through the redemption which is in Christ Jesus, whom God put forward as an expiation by his blood, to be received by faith. This was to show God's righteousness, because in his divine forbearance he has passed over former sins."

For us to be able to defeat the devil in this spiritual manipulation and brainwashing, we need to first be alert spiritually to know when this negative thoughts come into our mind, and the we need to start rebuking it, claiming the promises of God in order not to give room for such evil and negative words to take root in our mind and grow to destroying us.

God's promise says in (Romans 8:1-2) that,

"There is therefore now no condemnation for those who are in Christ Jesus, for the law of the spirit of life in Christ Jesus has set me free from the law of sin and death."

Believe only on the truth and the promise of God.

Prayer Points

Father, you said that,

"By thee I can crush a troop; and by my God I can leap over a wall. This God, his way is perfect; the promise of the Lord proves true; he is a shield for all those who take refuge in him." - (Psalms 18:29-30)

So Father, in your name I decree that every spiritual warfare and attack against my life and destiny is crushed and defeated forever in Jesus name. Amen.

It is written In (Psalm 27:1-3) that,

"The Lord is my light and my salvation; whom shall I fear? The Lord is the stronghold of my life; of whom shall I be afraid of? When evil doers assail me, uttering slanders against me, my adversaries and my foes, they shall stumble and fall."

Father, I pray that every conspiracy, manipulation and temptation against my life by the devil shall not succeed, and every plan shall stumble and fall in Jesus name. Amen.

It is written that,

"He who digs a pit will fall into it, and a stone will come back upon him who starts it rolling." - (Proverbs 26:27)

So Father, in the name of Jesus I decree that any one, people that plan any form of spiritual attack for me shall fall into the evil pit they have dug for me and perish in Jesus name. Amen.

It is written that,

"Therefore, God has highly exalted him and bestowed on him the name which is above every name, that at the name of Jesus every knee should bow, in heaven and on earth and under the earth, and every tongue confess that Jesus Christ is Lord, to the glory of God the Father." - (Philippians 2:9-11)

So today, I key into the power in the name of Jesus, and command that every evil power and manipulation in my life should bow and die in the name of Jesus. Amen.

It is written,

"For we are not contending against flesh and blood, but against the principalities, against the powers, against the world rulers of this present darkness, against the spiritual host of wickedness in the heavenly places." - (Ephesians 6:12)

Father, I know and believe that there is no power greater than you, for you are the supreme and sovereign God. So today I subject all the evil powers manipulating my life under you and I render them powerless and useless against me in Jesus name. Amen.

Father, In (John 10:10) your word says that,

"The thief comes only to steal and kill and destroy; I came that they may have life, and have it abundantly."

Father, in the name of Jesus, I come against any attack of the enemy meant to steal, kill and destroy my destiny, and I receive abundant grace and life from you in Jesus name. Amen.

It is written In (Romans 3:23) that,

"For all have sinned and fall short of the glory of God."

Father, I come today unto your throne of glory, and I pray that you forgive me of any sin that is giving the devil a foothold in my life. Redeem me and deliver me from all forms of spiritual attack by the devil in Jesus name. Amen.

Father, your word says in (Romans 8:1-2) that,

"There is therefore now no condemnation for those who are in Christ Jesus, for the law of the spirit of life in Christ Jesus has set me free from the law of sin and death."

So Father, by the power of the blood of Jesus that was shed on the cross of Calvary for me, I rebuke and terminate every form of condemnation that the devil is using to bring feeling of guilt and shame in my life, I set myself free now in Jesus name. Amen.

Father, I know that you are on my side, and that you have already answered all my prayers, because your word says in (Mark 11:24) that,

"Therefore I tell you, whatever you ask in prayer, believe that you have received it, and it will be yours."

Thank you Father, in Jesus name I pray, Amen.

Chapter 6: Forget The Past, Maximize The Future

A lot of people, even without knowing it, go about carrying the garbage of their past or mistake into their future, they carry into any new situation or relationship they go into, thereby hindering their capacity to be objective and see things from a positive and new perspective. The truth is that our past will never let us appreciate and maximize the future especially if they were negative and retrogressive.

In (Isaiah 43:18-19) the word of God says,

> ***"Remember not the former things, nor consider the things of old. Behold, I am doing a new thing; now it springs forth, do you not perceive it? I will make a way in the wilderness and rivers in the desert."***

Every single day that we get should be appreciated and seen as a gift, and a sign that the Almighty God desires above all things for us to live in peace and prosperity just as His word says in (3 John 2),

"Beloved, I wish above all things that thou mayest prosper and be in health, even as thy soul prospereth."

But a lot of people fail to achieve the level of success and prosperity that God desires for them because they allow the negativity, the mistakes, pains and failures from their past to determine the level of progress they can achieve, thereby limiting the new and glorious life that God intend to live.

Our past is powerful, and memories of the past are so powerful that they can shape our future; they can completely take control of our future and destroy it if the memory of the past is negative.

Even if the past was good and the memories sweet and pleasant, we should be careful how we bring it into the present and future if things are not the way we expect because they have the capacity to becloud our judgment and make us unable to appreciate the present and maximize the future.

God in His love and mercy has given each of us a divine destiny, so the choice is left to us to either pursue God's destiny or achieve success, or to let the mistakes, pains, failures and disappointment of the past determine our future.

In (Philippians 3:13:14),

> ***"Brethren, I do not consider that I have made it my own; but one thing I do, forgetting what lies behind and straining forward to what lies ahead. I press on toward the goal for the prize of the upward call of God in Christ Jesus."***

Apostle Paul's approach of looking forward and pressing towards the goal, instead of focusing on what lies behind and dwelling on the past, should be the way we Christians approach situations in times of adversity. A lot of people want to live in the present and maximize the future, but they don't have the capacity to let go of the negativity of the past, harness the opportunity in the present and enjoy the success that the future brings.

We must do everything possible and with the help of God to let go of the past if we desire to succeed in the future, because nothing will make the devil and the enemies of the children of God more happy than to see us trapped, constrained, and condemned by guilt, shame and failure of our past. The best way to overcome this and move forward is to fully accept the sacrifice that our Lord and savior Jesus Christ did for us when he died on the cross.

At the point of death on the cross, Jesus spoke three words that changed our lives forever, three words that take way all the mistakes, failures, pain, shame, disappointment and condemnation of the past. Jesus said, "IT IS FINISHED."

These three powerful words have transformed your dirty, filthy and negative past into a new and renewed you, for the word of God says in (2 Corinthians 5:17),

"If any man be in Christ, he is a new creature: old things are passed away, behold all things are become new."

So, stop holding on to the past, or living in the past, because the blood of Jesus that He shed for us on the cross of Calvary has wiped off our past.

Ways To Effectively Deal With The Past

- **Look At Yourself From God's Eyes**

  The devil always wants to remind the children of God of all the failures and mistakes that they have done in life.

  Failures and mistakes in their finances, marriage, educational pursuit and every other way they failed, and then the devil tries to paint a gloomy picture that these past mistakes and failures are so dirty and heavy that they can't amount to anything in life again or maximize their future.

  But that is not the true. God sees you as a success and not a failure. Stop trying to see yourself as a failure and as someone whose past is so bad that he can no longer make it in the future and start seeing yourself the way God sees you.

(2 Corinthians 5:17) says,

"Therefore if anyone is in Christ, he is a new creation, the old has passed away, behold, the new has come."

- **Allow God To Completely Heal Your Pain**

There is nothing that you can do on your own to completely wipe away the memory of your past mistakes and failures, or even the pains and regret that are holding you back from forgetting the past and maximizing the future.

The only solution to being able to put your past behind you, in order for it not to become a barrier holding you back, is to allow God come into your life and completely heal you and remove any negative chain in your life. Allow the spirit of the most High God to search deep into your heart in order to locate that area of your heart that is still hurting, and that is still bearing the shame, regrets, pains and disappointments of your past life so that He can perform the spiritual surgery of healing you completely.

Surrender your life to God, and God in His mercy will give you the grace to break away from the emotional and spiritual bondage that your past has held you to and give you the freedom to maximize the future.

- **Learn To Transform Your Past Mistakes Into Stepping Stones**

If you really want to leave your past behind and maximize your future, then you need to learn to transform your mistakes into valuable lessons that will positively shape the course of your future, instead of carrying it about everywhere you go and transferring it into your future.

When you don't effectively learn from your past and use them as a stepping stone to maximize your future, then you will keep repeating the mistakes of the past and fail to make meaningful progress.

Go to God in prayer, and ask Him to eliminate any stronghold that the mistakes and failures of the past have built in your life and for Him to give you the grace to move forward and maximize your future.

- **Live Above Regrets**

It is very important to live above regrets from failures and mistakes of the past if you want to maximize your future, because the longer you hold on to regrets the more you will keep on failing and experience more regrets.

You need as matter of urgency to break that negative vicious cycle of regret that is holding you from moving forward, by committing all the failures, pains and mistakes making you regret to God. Only God can wipe away the pain and sorrows of the past, and only He has the capacity to make whatever is bringing you regret to disappear and restore you back to the place you were destined to be.

You need to understand that no matter how long you dwell on the past, and hold on to what you have lost in the past, it will only drain you of the productive energy you need to move forward, but nothing will change, nor will your condition get better.

Know all the things that bring you pain and regret, and pray about them one after the other, asking God to heal your heart and give you the motivation to move forward and maximize your future.

Stop living in regret, and use the energy of that regret to drive you to the future you desire. The best way to overcome past mistakes and failure is not to live a life of regret, but to use them as the motivation you need to achieve success in the future

- **Learn To Forgive**

Sometimes, the past you are holding on to that is preventing you from moving forward and maximizing the future might be as a result of pain or disappointment caused by someone.

This makes you to bottle up offence or keep a grudge because of what has been done to you. But you have to know that keeping a grudge and holding offence is like carrying a heavy bag of garbage that will only pull you down, bring you bad and painful memories and deprive you of the needed joy and motivation to move forward.

So, you have to let go of grudges and offence, and forgive whoever has hurt you in the past, in order to let the weight of garbage off your shoulder and be free to objectively evaluate your present situation and achieve a favorable future.

- **God Can Still Use Us Despite Our Past**

A lot of people are so burdened and ashamed of their past that they go about with the mentality that they are not qualified to be used by God for the work of expanding His kingdom on earth.

When you give your life to God, and accept Jesus as your personal Lord and savior, His grace overwhelms you and qualifies you to do His will and function according to His purpose. In (Romans 5:2) that bible says,

"Through him we have obtained access to his grace in which we stand, and we rejoice in our hope of sharing the glory of God."

God can still use you for His good works despite how filthy, how dirty your past is, and despite the mistakes, the atrocities and the failures that characterized your past. You are a valuable asset and tool in the hand of God, and God created you for a specific purpose. You are unique and there is no replica of you that exists. So, no matter how guilty you feel about your past, because of all the mistakes that you have made, at the appointed time, God will single you out and use you to do that work He created you for.

In (Jeremiah 1:5), the word of God says,

"Before I formed you in the womb I knew you, before you were born I set you apart; I appointed you as a prophet to the nations."

(Micah 7:19) confirms it,

"Who is a God like thee, pardoning iniquity and passing over transgression for the remnant of his inheritance? He does not retain his anger forever because he delights in steadfast love. He will again have compassion on us, and he will tread our iniquities underfoot. Thou will cast all our sins into the depths of the sea."

Immediately you give your life to Christ, God wipes away your sins, your past and mistakes, so you become qualified to be an ambassador of God.

- **Accept Your Past And Move Forward**

Some people who have passed through pain, or experienced a loss or failure in their lives tend to do everything possible to suppress it, or live in denial. While this might bring you temporary relief, it is a very wrong approach to take.

The best thing to do when you have suffered loss or made a big mistake that brought failure and regret into your life is to fully accept that it has happened, and face the reality of what has happened. By so doing, you will discover new strength and a new motivation to live life again and maximize the future with what you have left.

Be free to discuss what happened to you, or what you have lost in the past with genuine friends and family members that love and truly care about you. That would help relieve you of the burden of the pain and sorrow and make you find happiness again.

The past and all its negative memories will keep affecting you and making you lose focus and direction if you don't accept it, and you will not have the power to let go and move forward if you are living in denial and don't want to accept what really happened to you. The truth is that if you are still struggling with, or refuse to accept the past, then your future can never be guaranteed. So you have to make peace with yourself and forget everything that has happened to you, and leave it in the past where it belongs.

- **Start Living In The Present**

The very moment that you accept what has happened to you and begin to live in the present, you will find peace, and you will become emotionally and physically free to see the opportunities that the present has for you, and if you are fully able to effectively harness those opportunities, then you can use them as a leverage to maximize your future.

Look into the present and count the abundant blessings that God has placed before you to recover all that you have lost and achieve your dreams. Embrace the present with joy and enthusiasm! Thank God for what is left in your life, and ask Him for the grace and wisdom to use what is left in the present to make your future better and brighter.

Your life and destiny is in the present and the future, and not in your past, so forget about it. The truth is that, except your aim is to praise God and glorify Him for all the good things that He has done in your life in the past, there is absolutely no need to dwell on worry about the future.

- **Move Into The Future With Hope And Excitement**

Once you have accepted the past, and start living positively in the present with all the opportunities it presents, then you have to move into the future with hope, expectations and excitement.

Don't be afraid of the future, but move into it with hope and faith that the God who kept you and gave you the grace to go through all the difficulties of the past will position you for a great and prosperous future. God will never fail or abandon His children because He is so concerned about their future, and He has promised to make their future great and prosperous. In (Jeremiah 29:11-12) the word of God says,

"For I know the plans I have for you, says the Lord, plans for welfare and not for evil, to give you a future and a hope. Then you will call upon me and come and pray to me, and I will hear you."

God desires a good future for you, but all you have to do is call upon Him and He will give you the future you desire. In (1 Corinthians 2:9) the bible tells us that,

"What no eye has seen, no ear hear has heard, nor the heart of man conceived, that is what God has prepared for those who love Him."

The future has a lot of hope if you move into it with excitement and believing that there is nothing that God can't do. For the bible gives us this assurance in (Ephesians 3:20-21) when it says

"Now to him who by the power at work within us is able to do far more abundantly than all that we ask or think, to him be the glory in the church and in Christ Jesus to all generations, forever and ever, Amen."

These are some ways that we hold on to the past and we need to avoid them

Not Asking God For Help

Some people know that they are completely broken, and that the negativity from their past is holding them back from appreciating the present and maximising the future, yet out of pride and unbelief they refuse to seek the help of God.

And it is only out of God's mercy and grace that we can completely get the healing that we need to forget the past and move into the glorious future that God destined for us. So ask God for help today, remove your pride and be humble, and God will heal your past, for God's word said in (2 Chronicles 7:14),

"If my people who are called by my name humble themselves, and pray and seek my face and turn from their wicked ways, then I will hear from heaven and I will forgive their sin and heal their land."

Not Asking For Help From Our Destiny Helpers And Friends

The truth is that no man is an island, and there are people that God have destined to help us in times of need, and God has given us some genuine and caring friends, but pride sometimes hold us back from asking these people for help.

Asking for help when you feel lost, and when it seems like the whole world is crashing down on you is nothing to be ashamed of. We can talk to our spiritual fathers or elders in our church and ask for their help, by so doing the burdens in our life can get lifted or reduced.

Start To Live In Isolation

Living in isolation, or avoiding people because of the problems in our life, and the mistakes, failures, pains and disappointment of our past will only worsen the situation, make us depressed, and deprive us the motivation needed to live happily in the present and maximize the future.

Holding On To Shame And Disgrace Of The Past

Some people's minds have been so affected by the shame and disgrace of the past that believe they have no right to be happy, or qualified to do anything meaningful to make their future glorious.

They have this negative mindset that anything they do again will end up in shame and disgrace just like before, so they stop living, they stop aspiring, they stop dreaming and automatically though they are alive, but emotionally and psychologically dead.

Prayer Points

Father, your word says In (Isaiah 43:18-19),

> ***"Remember not the former things, nor consider the things of old. Behold, I am doing a new thing; now it springs forth, do you not perceive it? I will make a way in the wilderness and rivers in the desert."***

So Father, in the name of Jesus I pray for the grace not to live in the past, and let my past be a burden that will hinder me from achieving greatness in the future. I receive all the new great things you are doing in my life in Jesus name. Amen.

Father, your word said in (3 John 2),

> ***"Beloved, I wish above all things that thou mayest prosper and be in health, even as thy soul prospereth."***

Father, I key into your in (3 John 2), and I decree in the name of Jesus that my past no matter how dirty it had been will not deprive me of the prosperity in my health and health and finances that you have promised me in Jesus name. Amen.

It is written in (Philippians 3:13:14) that,

> **"Brethren, I do not consider that I have made it my own; but one thing I do, forgetting what lies behind and straining forward to what lies ahead. I press on toward the goal for the prize of the upward call of God in Christ Jesus."**

Father, I humbly come unto your throne of glory, asking for your help to completely forget what lies behind, and for you to give me strength to move ahead in life and achieve the great goals that lies ahead of me in Jesus name. Amen.

Father, your word says in (2 Corinthians 5:17) that,

> **"If anyone is in Christ, he is a new creation, the old has passed away, behold, the new has come."**

So Father, I thank you for sending your only begotten Son to die for me, and today I receive the blood of Jesus to wipe away all my dirty and filthy past, and to receive the newness in Christ Jesus. Amen.

Father, your word says in (Jeremiah 1:5) that,

"Before I formed you in the womb I knew you, before you were born I set you apart; I appointed you as a prophet to the nations."

I believe you Father, and I decree that any contrary voice from my past that is trying to destroy your divine plan and purpose for my life shall perish and die in Jesus name. Amen.

It is written in (Micah 7:19) that,

"Who is a God like thee, pardoning iniquity and passing over transgression for the remnant of his inheritance?"

Father, I thank you for forgiving the mistakes, sins and iniquity of my past, and now that I am a new man in Christ Jesus, I pray for the divine speed to recover all I lost in the past due to sin, and the wisdom to maximize my future in Jesus name.

Father, you said in (Jeremiah 29:11),

> **"For I know the plans I have for you, says the Lord, plans for welfare and not for evil, to give you a future and a hope."**

Father, I believe your word and promise, and I refuse to settle for less. May your grace lead me so that all the plans, hope and future you have for me will not be delayed or destroyed by the mistakes of my past in Jesus name. Amen.

It is written in (1 Corinthians 2:9) that,

> **"What no eye has seen, no ear heard, nor the heart of man conceived, what God has prepared for those who love Him."**

Father, I thank you for you are a glorious God, I exalt your Holy name because you are a God that decrees and promises and it comes to pass. Father, I pray that all your promises and all the things you have prepared for me will come to pass in my life in Jesus name. Amen.

It is written in (Ephesians 3:20),

"Now to him who by the power at work within us is able to do far more abundantly than all that we ask or think."

Father, I know that you can do all things, so I pray that in any way that the mistake of my past is hindering me from getting favor from you and from my destiny helpers, may that situation change now in Jesus name. Amen.

Chapter 7: No Condition Is Permanent

The world was actually created by God to be a beautiful place, filled with joy, laughter and prosperity, but due to the sinful nature of man, the world has become a place filled with uncertainty, ups and down and other conditions of life those were not actually part of God's plan when He was creating the world.

The world we live in now is in phases and conditions, because there are people living a life of lack, poverty, sickness and crisis, while some are living a happy and fulfilled life.

But whatever condition you are in right now, the most deciding and most important is the condition that you will be in tomorrow, because there is no condition in life that is permanent.

So, the condition that you are facing at this particular moment might be that of pain, poverty, suffering, sickness, anguish, anxiety, or any adverse condition, but you should not despair, lose hope, blame others, or even yourself for the condition you find yourself, but rather commit your life and everything into the hands of God, and you will see that your tomorrow will far better than your today.

The Bible says in (Psalms 30:5),

"Weeping may endure for a night, but joy comes in the morning."

All you need do is have faith in God that He will bring hope, sunshine and joy into that your condition that looks gloomy today. "When there is life, there is hope," it is said. And this is true for everyone that is alive and breathing. There is no condition in your life that you can't change or surmount with dedication, hard work, diligence, perseverance and faith in God.

There is nothing you can't accomplish, there is no goal you set your mind on that you can't attain, as long as you are alive and hopeful. It doesn't really matter your present condition, or the position you are right now, know and believe that the only permanent thing in life is change. So, work hard and be prayerful, and the wind of change will blow away that negative condition in your life and replace it with hope, favor, greatness and God's abundant blessings.

The condition, or the phase you are in today, is not the indication of what your life will look like tomorrow. We are not like people of the world that puts all their focus on what they see, and judge by the physical things that they see, but as children of the Most High God, we live by faith not sight, for the things that the eyes can see are just temporary things, but eternal and long lasting things are unseen.

The bible says that faith is,

"The assurance of things hoped for, the conviction of things not seen." - (Hebrews 11:1)

As God's children, we should endeavor to walk by faith at all times, and not by sight of the present situation. God's promises of how He is going to redeem, strengthen and restore you to a level of glory and prosperity abound.

Consequently, if you have experienced a great loss, and you feel that your situation will never get better again, you need to change such negative mindset, and develop confidence in God that you will overcome your present situation and receive complete restoration.

In (Joel 2:25-26), the word of God promises complete restoration of your circumstances and whatever you have lost. It says,

> *"I will restore to you the years that the swarming locust has eaten, the crawling locust, the consuming locust, and the chewing locust, my great army which I sent among you. You shall eat in plenty and be satisfied, and praise the name of Lord your God, who has dealt wondrously with you; and my people shall never be put to shame."*

The phases of life are temporary and not permanent. A typical case is the story of Joseph in the Bible. At one point, we saw that Joseph was a happy young man who was well loved and favored by his father, but all of a sudden he became a slave as he was sold by his brothers to slave traders who sold him to an Egyptian master (Potiphar).

In Potiphar's house, Joseph found favor again, and everything looked like it was back to normal, or even better, because his master put him in charge of the other slaves and everything that he had. But when it seemed like Joseph was enjoying his new position, another phase of life came. This time he was wrongly accused of a crime he did not commit and sent to jail in a foreign land.

Joseph went from a well beloved and favored son, to a slave, and then to a prisoner. For some of us, it will feel like the end of the world has come for us, so we lose hope and even wish for death, but not so with Joseph. He kept on trusting and believing God, and having faith that, that was not the end of his life, and that the condition he found himself was not permanent. And with the help of God, Joseph's condition changed from that of a prisoner to a prince, as he was made second in command to Pharaoh, the king of Egypt.

You see, no condition is permanent. Life is a precious gift from God, and we treasure it and know that God is aware of any condition we are passing through, and He is more than able to change it at any time just as he did for Joseph.

There is a popular saying which goes, "When there is life, there is hope." And it is a fact of life because as long as you are still alive and breathing, there is no situation in your life that God can't change.

There are people going through sweet and favorable conditions right now. People living the life of affluence and plenty, they should thank God and give glory to His Holy name and not assume that their strength and intelligence made them different from others, or underrate and despise people that are living in lack and poverty now, because tomorrow is pregnant and loaded with surprises, for someone that is rich today can become poor tomorrow and vice versa.

The Bible says in (Ecclesiastes 9:11),

"Again I saw that under the sun the race is not to the swift, nor the battle to the strong, nor bread to the wise, nor riches to the intelligent, nor favor to the men of skill, but time and chance happen to them all."

Life is unpredictable. Our tomorrow is not carved in stone neither do we have the power to determine what will happen in our life tomorrow. Yes, we can plan for tomorrow, but the very best we can do is pray and hope that all our plans come true.

Do not carry yourself so proudly, and assume that because you are well placed and rich that things will definitely continue like that. There is no need to be proud and conceited, or look down on other people because they are not as healthy, rich and prosperous as you are. Your strength, intelligence and wisdom did not make you better than the other person, but time, chance and opportunity in life placed you above him.

And because no condition is permanent, and phases and situations in life can change at any time, the person you regard as a failure, that person you regard as poor and unsuccessful can have the time, chance and opportunity that you have today, and everything about their life will be transformed.

Life is in the hands of God, and the Bible makes us to know that,

"Every good gift and every perfect gift is from above, and cometh down from the Father of lights, with who is no variableness, neither shadow of turning."
- (James 1:17)

So, don't boast in your own strength and capability because everything you own was given to you by God, and that same God that gave you those gifts, can do same in the life of other people. A rich man today can become a pauper tomorrow, and a pauper can become rich. The man that his soul is cast down and depressed today, can be revived by God to live a life of joy and happiness, and the one with so much joy and happiness can become sad and depressed tomorrow. The man that is suffering from all forms of crisis and adversity today might become a whole and fulfilled man tomorrow.

You just need to maintain a positive and hopeful outlook in life, and know that your Father in heaven holds the key to your life and He has the power to change that awful condition you are in today, and transform your life for good. In (Psalms 42:5) the Bible says,

"Why are thou cast down, O my soul? And why are though disquieted in me? Hope thou in God, for I shall yet praise him for the help of his countenance."

You don't need to despair, or kill yourself with worry just because things are not moving exactly the way you plan. That is the attitude of those who don't know God, and don't believe in His power to make a way where there seems to be no way, and make everything perfect in His appointed time.

So, wait and rely on your God, and He will surely transform your situation. In (Isaiah 40:31) the word of God says,

"But those that wait upon the Lord shall renew their strength; they shall mount up the wings as eagles; they shall run, and not be weary; and they shall walk, and not faint."

God has deposited so much potential in all that He created, and if at this particular time you have not been able to maximize the potential that God has blessed you with and live the life you so desire, don't fret or be afraid, or write yourself off that you are finished, or even believe what people say about you, but dig deep and use that talent that God has given you and your condition in life will change. Put all your trust in God, and look up to Him to change all negative and devastating situations in your life.

For the Bible says,

"Looking unto Jesus, the author and finisher of our faith, who for the joy that

was set before Him endured the cross, despising the shame, and he sat down at the right hand of the throne of God." - (Hebrews 12:2)

Prayer Points

Father, thank you for my condition today, I thank you Father for I have the faith and assurance in you and in your promises that my condition today will change for the better. Despite how my condition is right now, my faith in you is unshakable, because it is written that,

"Faith is the assurance of things hoped for, the conviction of things not seen." - (Hebrews 11:1)

Thank you Father, in Jesus name I pray. Amen.

It is written that,

"Every good gift and every perfect gift is from above, and cometh down from the Father of lights, with who is no variableness, neither shadow of turning." - (James 1:17)

So Father, I believe in your word, and believe that the perfect gift, the perfect condition that you desire for me must surely come to pass in Jesus name. Amen.

Father, your word says in (Psalms 42:5) that,

"Why are thou cast down, O my soul? And why are though disquieted in me? Hope though in God, for I shall yet praise him for the help of his countenance."

So Father, in the name of Jesus, I rebuke all forms of sadness and depression that have plagued my life because of my condition, and put my complete hope in you, for in you I shall rejoice and be happy again in Jesus name. Amen.

Father, your word says in (Psalms 30:5) that,

"Weeping may endure for a night, but joy comes in the morning."

Father, any condition in my life that is bringing pain and weeping in my life, in the powerful name of Jesus I banish it from my life, and I receive joy, peace and prosperity in Jesus name. Amen.

It is written in (Isaiah 40:31) that,

"But those that wait upon the Lord shall renew their strength; they shall mount up the wings as eagles; they shall run, and not be weary; and they shall walk, and not faint."

Father, despite the severity of my condition, I pray for the strength and grace to wait for your appointed time for my healing and restoration, rather than depending on evil sources, in Jesus name, Amen.

Father, you said in (Joel 2:25),

"I will restore to you the years that the swarming locust has eaten, the crawling locust, the consuming locust, and the chewing locust, my great army which I sent among you."

So Father, I pray for your divine restoration, restoration in my health, restoration in my finance and restoration in anything that has made my condition in life painful and unfavorable in Jesus name. Amen.

Father, you said in (Joel 2:26) that,

"You shall eat in plenty and be satisfied, and praise the name of Lord your God, who has dealt wondrously with you; and my people, shall never be put to shame."

Father, in the name of Jesus, I decree that every condition of lack and scarcity in my life shall turn to plenty, and you shall give me satisfaction in everything that I do and I shall come back with thanksgiving and praise in Jesus name. Amen.

It is written in (Ecclesiastes 9:11) that,

"Again I saw that under the sun the race is not to the swift, nor the battle to the strong, nor bread to the wise, nor riches to the intelligent, nor favor to the men of skill, but time and chance happen to them all."

Father, I plead for your mercy and protection because I have no power to change my condition, and I commit my life into your able hands, have mercy on me and transform my condition for good in Jesus name. Amen.

Father, thank you for answering all my prayers, I have faith that my condition has turned favorable and perfect because I have put all my hope and trust in Jesus,

"The author and finisher of our faith." - (Hebrews 12:2)

Thank you Father, in Jesus name I pray, Amen.

Chapter 8: Faith In Times Of Life Challenges

Every one of us has passed, or is passing through a difficult time in life right now. The difficult situation that you are currently passing through might be as a result of losing a loved one, financial crisis, marital crisis, loss of job, or a serious health condition that seems to have defiled all forms of treatment and left you financially bankrupt and hopeless.

No matter what the situation is, you should be rest assured that there is someone that knows exactly what you are going through, and He is willing and able to turn your situation around and completely restore to you all that you have lost, and that person is God, your Redeemer, He knows all about you, all you have to do is commit your situation into His able hands and have faith that He can handle it. The truth is that whatever you are going through right now might be very hard and difficult for you, but our God is a good God.

The Bible says in (Deuteronomy 31:6),

"Be strong and of good courage, do not fear or be in dread of them; for it is the Lord who goes with you, he will not fail you or forsake you."

So, it is high time you moved from the point of feeling defeated and being a victim of the situation you are passing through, to start trusting God and finding purpose for your life through faith in God.

(Romans 8:35-39) says,

"Who shall separate us from the love of Christ? Shall tribulation, or distress, or persecution, or famine, or nakedness, or peril, or sword? As it is written 'For thy sake we are being killed all day long; we are regarded as sheep to be slaughtered. No in all these things we are more than conquerors through him who loved us. For I am sure that neither death, nor life, nor angels, nor principalities, nor things present, nor things to come, nor powers,

nor heights, nor depth, nor anything else in all creation, will be able to separate us from the love of God in Christ Jesus our Lord."

That is how much God loves, so no matter what the situation is, have faith in His love through Christ Jesus that the situation will pass and His glory will shine through you. The Scripture says you are more than a conqueror. Stop parading yourself as a defeated victim of your circumstance, and start experiencing the love that God has for you through faith, because there is no circumstance or situation that will separate you from His love.

How To Develop Faith In Times Of Challenges

- **Open Your Heart To God**

  When you are going through difficult times, and it looks like the situation is too much to bear that is the right time to surrender to God and give the Holy Spirit room to come into your life and work the perfect will of God concerning your situation.

When you open your heart to God, you need to guard the thought of your heart and the words that come out of your mouth, so that you will not be working contrary to the will of God for your life.

You need to speak words of faith and victory, not fear and defeat. If the Holy Spirit is saying you are a conqueror through Christ Jesus, and you are confessing that you are a defeated victim, there is no way that God's perfect will can be fulfilled in your life.

So, when you are experiencing tough and difficult situation, the first step to receiving healing and restoration into your life, is to guide the thought of your heart and the words that come out from your mouth. Your confessions of faith in times of difficulty and adversity will determine the level of God's move you will provoke in your life.

(Proverbs 4:23-24) says,

***"Keep your heart with all vigilance;
for from it flows the spring of life.
Put away crooked speech and put
devious talks far from you."***

This verse makes us understand that the positive thoughts and words we confess when we are passing through difficult times, will determine how God will intervene in our situation, so we need to be careful with what we think and say.

Open your heart in faith today and say this prayer in faith. Father, King of glory, the God that rules in the affairs of men. Father your word says that,

"That though desirest in the inward being; therefore teach me wisdom in my secret heart." - (Psalm 51:6)

So, today I ask in faith for you to open my heart to receive the gift of the Holy Spirit, and guide my heart and thought to be in line with your will and purpose for my life in Jesus name I pray. Amen.

- **Hold On Strongly To God's Word**

The Bible says,

> ***"Faith comes by hearing, and hearing by the word of God." - (Romans 10:17)***

If you want to build your faith in times of difficulty, you have to hold on strongly and meditate on the word of God at all times. In (Joshua 1:8) the Bible says,

> ***"Keep this book of the Law always on your lips; meditate on it day and night, so that you may be careful to do everything written in it. Then you will be prosperous and successful."***

The word of God contains His promises, precepts and the hope we need to overcome difficult situations, so meditate on the word and key into God's promises in faith and you will find the peace, hope and joy to overcome difficult situations. Holding on and meditating on God's word builds up your faith in times of trouble, because it opens your eyes to God promises.

- **Prayer**

  Prayer increases your faith in times of trouble. Prayer helps you to communicate with God, and in doing so, you fellowship and develop a personal relationship with Him.

  During prayer, your faith for the things of God is ignited, and you will receive the outpouring of the Holy Spirit which gives you the strength and peace of mind to overcome whatever situation you may be facing at that point in time. Spend valuable time praying and connecting to God. And when praying, endeavor to ask God to do His will, and what He knows is best for you, and not what you think is the best for you.

  Pray for the Holy Spirit to make all your prayers and petitions to align with the will and purpose of God for your life. Prayer builds faith, and faith is the only thing that God responds to in times of trials and tribulation.

- **Your Mind Needs To Be Renewed**

For you to develop and effectively practice the type of faith that moves mountains and deal with the problems in your life, you need to renew your mind and change your attitude about the way you see the things of God and the promises that He has made concerning your life.

In (Romans 12:2), the Bible says,

> *"Do not be conformed to this world, but be transformed by the renewal of your mind, that you may prove what is the will of God, what is good and acceptable and perfect."*

The way we think, and the way we program our mind to react in times of crisis and trouble determine the type of faith we will have when confronting that situation.

We need to renew our mind and the way we think to be in line with what God thinks about us, because a negative and defeatist mindset will make you to fall completely out of line with the will of God for your life. Renew your mind concerning what the world says or thinks about the situation and problems in your life, and start believing what God says about that situation and you will see your faith grow and become strong.

The Bible says,

"Faith is the assurance of things hoped for, the conviction of things not seen." - (Hebrews 11:1)

And there is no way you can have faith that the things you hoped for will come to pass if you don't renew your mind.

- **Be Thankful And Praise God Always**

Thanksgiving and praise to God helps us to grow and strengthen our faith in God, and when this happens, there is no situation that we will face that we will not surmount and overcome.

The Bible says in (1 Thessalonians 5:18),

"Give thanks in all circumstances; for this is God's will for you in Christ Jesus."

Our heavenly Father wants us to thank Him, and give praise to His name at all times and more so in times of need. As you do so, your faith is reinforced, and you are transformed from adversity to the realm where you experience the power, love and awesome goodness of God.

When your faith is reinforced, how you see your situation will change,. You will no longer see despair and hopelessness, but the power of the Most High God that is able to transform you from hopelessness to joy.

It makes God happy when His beloved children are praising Him even in their midst of trials and tribulations, because it proves that we have surrendered everything to Him, and have faith in His ability to heal and restore us.

The Bible says in (Hebrews 11:6),

"Without faith it is impossible to please him. For whoever will draw near to God must believe that he exist and he rewards those who seek him."

Satan is the architect of all adversity that befall the children of God, so when you show him that you still have faith in God by giving thanks and praising the name of God, he will run away from you with all the garbage that goes with him.

- **Endeavor To Nurture Your Soul And Spirit**

Edify and nurture your soul and spirit in order to find the faith you need to stand firm and persevere in times of trials and tribulations.

In (1 Thessalonians 5:23) the Bible says,

> ***"May the God of peace himself sanctify your body, and may your spirit and soul and body be kept sound and blameless at the coming of our Lord Jesus Christ."***

When you are going through adversity, most especially if the situation takes a very long time, it breaks down your body, and takes a heavy toll on your soul and spirit, and makes it very difficult to maintain faith, so you need to pray fervently, for God to give you the grace to build back the faith you need to trust in Him and persevere in times of need. Endeavor to nurture your soul and spirit by speaking words of faith and truth into your spirit, and declaring the promises of God concerning whatever situation you are passing through.

- **Rely On Your Faith, Not How You Feel**

Our faith, not our feelings, is what matters to God. We need to totally believe God's promises for our life, and believe that God is in total control of any circumstance that we are passing through.

God's love for us is total and complete, so we should endeavor not to let our feelings become an obstacle to receiving from God, and accessing His promise for us. When we are passing through trials and tribulations, our feelings are quite erratic and unreliable; we experience mood swings. That mean we can't make decisions based in our feelings in times of adversity, or to use in judging if God is on our side or not.

In times of trials and tribulation, anchor your decisions on faith and the truth of God's word about His goodness, the reliability and the capacity of the Holy Spirit to handle the situation and comfort you with the needed hope and joy to face your situation and come out victorious. Always pray to receive the faith that is needed to believe and stand firm on the promises of God, and be vigilant because the devil will want to manipulate your emotions and feelings in order to deceive you that God doesn't care about you and what you are going through.

I know you might be going through a lot of pain and suffering due to what you are passing through, but instead of expending all your energy on your suffering, try instead to get some valuable lessons from your situations and grow from it.

- **Stop Asking Why, And Ask God How**

The truth is that no matter the situation you are passing through right now, no matter how painful or hard it is, asking God why will not build your faith in Him, it will weaken you; diminish your faith in God, and His promises.

And if you expect that God will answer your "WHY ME" questions, you will only leave yourself in disappointment, because God is under no obligation to reveal the reasons why you are going through what you are going through. The best approach to build your faith, restore your confidence in God, and the type that God responds to is when you ask God ''HOW.'' That is asking God how to faithfully react to the trials and tribulations that you are passing through.

When you do this, God will respond because He knows that you trust Him, so He will reveal to you the purpose of that situation and what you need to do to overcome it. In faith and complete trust in Him, ask how God intends to use the situation that you are going through to draw you more close to Him and fulfill His purpose for your life.

Inspiring Bible Quotes To Help You Find Faith In Times Of Trouble

- *"Do not fear, for I am with you; do not be dismayed, for I am your God. I will strengthen you and help you; I will uphold you with my righteous right hand." - (Isaiah 41:10)*

- *"The righteous cry out, and the Lord hears them, he delivers them from all troubles. The Lord is close to the brokenhearted and saves those who are crushed in spirit." - (Psalms 34:17-18)*

- *"But he said to me my grace is sufficient for you, for my power is made perfect in weaknesses. Therefore I will boast all the more gladly about my weakness, so that Christ's power may rest on me. That is why, for Christ's sake, I delight in weakness, in insults, in hardships, in persecutions, in difficulties. For when I am weak, then I am strong." - (2 Corinthians 12:9-10)*

- *"But now thus says the Lord, he who created you, O Jacob, he who formed you, O Israel: Fear not, for I have redeemed you; I have called you by name, you are mine. When you pass through the waters I will be with you; and through the rivers, they shall not overwhelm you; when you walk through fire you shall not be burned, and the flame shall not consume you, for I am the Lord your God, the Holy One of Israel, your Savior. I give Egypt as your ransom, Ethiopia and Sheba in exchange for you." - (Isaiah 43:1-3)*

- *"Therefore we do not lose heart. Though outwardly we are wasting away, yet inwardly we are being renewed day by day. For our light and momentary troubles are achieving for us an eternal glory that far outweighs them all. So we fix our eyes not on what is seen, but on what is unseen, since what is seen is temporary, but what is unseen is eternal." - (2 Corinthians 4:16-18)*

- *"Do you not know? Have you not heard? The Lord is the everlasting God, the Creator of the ends of the earth. He will not go tired or weary, and his understanding no one can fathom. He gives strength to the weary and increases the power of the weak. Even youths grow tired and weary, and young men stumble and fall; but those who hope in the Lord will renew their strength. They will soar on wings like eagles; they will run and not grow weary, they will walk and not be faint." - (Isaiah 40:28-31)*

- *"But the Advocate, The Holy Spirit, whom the Father will send in my name, will teach you all things and will remind you of everything I have said to you. Peace I live with you; my peace I give you. I do not give to you as the world gives. Do not let your hearts be troubled and do not be afraid." - (John 14:26-27)*

- *"Dear friends, do not be surprised at the fiery ordeal that has come on to test you, as though something strange has happened to you. But rejoice inasmuch as you participate in the sufferings of Christ, so that you may be overjoyed when his glory is revealed." - (1 Peter 4:12-13)*

Prayer Points

Father, your word says that,

"Faith comes by hearing, and hearing by the word of God." - (Romans 10:17)

So Father, I plead for the strength and grace to read and meditate on your words in order to build up my faith in times of life challenges, in Jesus name. Amen.

Father, in (Proverbs 4:23-24) your word says,

"Keep your heart with all vigilance; for from it flows the spring of life. Put away crooked speech and put devious talks far from you."

Father, I pray for the wisdom and understanding to use positive life changing words in time of challenges. Words that bring healing and restoration, in Jesus name. Amen.

It is written in (Joshua 1:8),

"Keep this book of the law always on your lips; meditate on it day and night, so that you may be careful to do everything

written in it. Then you will be prosperous and successful."

Father, I thank you and praise your Holy name, for success and prosperity comes only from you. Give me the grace to keep your law in order to avoid any form of challenge that will deprive me from enjoying success and prosperity in Jesus name. Amen.

It is written in (1 Thessalonians 5:18),

"Give thanks in all circumstances; for this is God's will for you in Christ Jesus."

Father, build up my faith, and lead me through the path of understanding, the type of faith and understanding that will make me to give thanks and praise your name in all circumstances, in Jesus name. Amen.

Father, your word says in (Hebrews 11:6) that,

"Without faith it is impossible to please him. For whoever will draw near to God must believe that he exist and he rewards those who seek him."

Father, I know that I can only get access to you and receive from you through faith, so I plead that anything that is making me faithless and afraid should die by fire in Jesus name. Amen.

It is written in (Romans 8:35) that,

"Who shall separate us from the love of Christ? Shall tribulation, or distress, or persecution, or famine, or nakedness, or peril, or sword?"

Father, king of glory, the creator of heaven and earth, the unchangeable changer, God of love and prosperity, I thank you for the strong love you have for me, I thank you because there is no force strong enough to separate me from your love. Thank you for your love has defeated my life challenges in Jesus name. Amen.

Father, your word says,

"Do not fear, for I am with you; do not be dismayed, for I am your God. I will strengthen you and help you; I will uphold you with my righteous right hand." - (Isaiah 41:10)

Father, I thank you for your promise to be with me always, I praise your name for your promise has built up my faith in you in times of challenges. Thank you for upholding with your righteous right hand in Jesus name. Amen.

Father, your word says,

"My grace is sufficient for you, for my power is made perfect in weaknesses." - (2 Corinthians 12:9)

So Father, I thank you for your abundant and sufficient grace in times of life challenges, I thank you for your power has made me perfect and strong when I was weak, Father, glory, honor and adoration be to your name forever in Jesus name. Amen.

Father, my God, my light and salvation, the stronghold of my life, I thank you for answering all my prayers. I thank you for in faith I know that you have defeated all my life challenges and set me free in Jesus name. Amen.

Chapter 9: How To Triumph Over Life Challenges

Challenges are a part of human life. But a lot of people find it difficult to accept the challenges they face in life, which makes it difficult for them to effectively deal and triumph over their challenges. Life is not a bed of roses. Things will not always go as we plan them to be, so we should be prepared to deal with the challenges that life will throw at us.

The truth about life is that challenges will come in various ways and forms such as in our finances, career, personal relations, marriage, health, etc. But many people are overwhelmed by these challenges, get afraid to handle it, or give up while trying, which makes the challenges to defeat them.

Here's how to effectively triumph over life's challenges:

Accept The Reality Of The Situation And Face It

When you are facing a difficult challenge in life, the first thing you need to do in order to effectively deal with it and triumph over it, is to accept the reality of the present situation that you find yourself, and face that situation without fear.

If you don't accept the present reality of the challenges that you are facing, you will live in denial, which denies you the strength and motivation you need to triumph over your challenges.

Change is a constant thing in the life of man, so when a new change in the form of a challenge comes, we should endeavor to accept it and deal with it.

Depression, despair and frustration come into your life when you refuse to face reality, and hold on to the past when things were good and comfortable. Accepting the present reality in our life, enables us to see the situation from a more positive perspective, which makes us remain calm while assessing the situation and knowing the best way to effectively deal with it and triumph over it.

See Yourself As Success

In (Numbers 13:32b-33), we saw the reaction of some of the Israelite spies sent to spy on the land of Canaan, and the negative report they brought back even though God was with them and have delivered them from many battles.

They said,

"The land through which we have gone, to spy out, is a land that devours its inhabitants, and all the people that we saw in it, are men of great stature. And there we saw the Nephilim (The sons of Anak who came from the Nephilim), and we seemed like to ourselves like grasshoppers, and so we seemed to them."

This is exactly the mentality of a lot Christians whenever they are going through a very difficult challenge, or when they are faced with obstacle. Out of fear, they forget what God has done for them in the past, the battles He has fought for them and the victories won.

But Joshua and Caleb had a different mentality, they believed that the God they served was well able to give them victory and help them triumph over their enemy hence they said,

"Let us go up at once and occupy it; for we are well able to overcome it." - (Numbers 13:30)

The language of Joshua and Caleb is the language of faith, the faith that every child of God needs to triumph over all the challenges in life. We need to understand that God has an awesome purpose for our life. In (Psalms 139:14) the bible says,

"I praise you, for I am fearfully and wonderfully made."

But the truth is that you will not achieve the purpose of God in your life, or have the grace and strength to achieve victory and triumph over your life challenges unless you start seeing yourself as God sees you.

Take Your Focus Away From The Challenge, And Focus It On God

The size of your challenge might be greater than you, but it is certainly not greater than God, so if you want to triumph over your problem and achieve your desired victory, then you need to stop focusing on how difficult, and how big the challenge is and start focusing on how big God is.

In (Jeremiah 32:27) the bible says,

> *"Behold, I am the Lord, the God of all flesh, is anything too hard for me?"*

The answer is no, nothing is too hard for God to do, and that includes the present challenge that you are facing. It is not too big for God. Your attention, therefore, should be on the God that can do all things and not on your challenge. God is ever ready and willing to help you triumph over any challenge you are going through right now, but all you need to do is focus on the awesome power of the Most High God, and you will start to see that your challenge as surmountable, and with the help of God, you will overcome it and come out triumphant.

Be aware and confident that the God who created you, and kept you alive up to this stage is fully aware of everything that is happening in your life, and he loves you and want to help you overcome it.

Begin now to see that challenge in your life as a great opportunity to build a lasting relationship with God and to cultivate the faith you need in times of challenge. Trust in the Lord to hold your hand, and lead you to the path of victory.

Don't Play The Blame Game

The truth is that the challenges that you are facing now is already a reality of your present life, so no matter how long you take in blaming others, or blaming yourself, the longer you will remain hurt by the situation.

Learn to take full responsibility for your problems, and don't be in the habit of looking for people to blame for your current situation, because blaming others for what they did to you that led to your challenges is like saying they are in control of your life, which they are not.

God is the only one that has complete control of your life, so instead of blaming others, or even yourself for the challenges in your life, commit that challenge to God, and ask Him to give you the strength and wisdom to overcome your challenge and triumph over it.

Seek Help From Other Believers

The Bible tells us that there is no affliction that is common to man. That means no matter the size and the difficulty of the challenge that you are passing through right now, someone else has experienced it before, or knows someone that had experienced it.

Seek help from other believers that have an idea about your present challenge, and with the help of God, they might be able to give you godly advice that will encourage, strengthen and help you triumph over your challenge.

Don't make the mistake of isolating yourself as that will only worsen the situation and delay your healing. Instead seek help and support from others.

The three sources of support that a child of God should explore in times of challenge are first, from God by humbly opening your heart and release all the burdens of your challenge into His able hands. Tell God about all the challenges that you are struggling with, your fears and worries about the challenges and ask him to take the burdens off you and to give you strength to triumph over the challenges.

Secondly, seek help in the household of God. Let your brethren know the challenges you are going through and what you need. The needs might be in the form of finance and material support, emotional, psychological or spiritual support in the form of prayer and counseling.

Thirdly, we can look inward and support ourselves. This is very important because no matter any form of support you get from God and man, and your spirit refuses to accept and work with it, there is no way you are going to triumph over the challenges you are facing.

We help ourselves by first believing the promises of God about the challenge we are going through, and then start speaking the word of faith and encouragement into our lives and into that situation.

Make Daily And Consistent Progress

No matter the level of the challenge you are going through, one of the surest way to overcome it is to not give up. Do everything possible, and by the help of God make daily and consistent progress toward overcoming the challenge and celebrating your triumph.

Wake up daily with hope, and ask the Holy Spirit to guide you through the steps you need to take for that day in order to come closer to defeating your challenge.

If you make any step and it doesn't go as you planned, don't give up or get frustrated, because it is only through making daily consistent steps that you can achieve the victory you desire and triumph over difficult challenges.

Obedience To God's Word Will Lead To Triumph

The challenge you are going through might be hard, painful and very difficult, but the best way to receive the blessing of God and achieve the triumph you desire in times of challenge is to diligently obey the word of God.

Despite how hard the challenge is, if you hearken diligently to the word of God, He will surely reward you for obeying Him. When you keep faith in God, and obey even when it seems difficult, God will position you for victory, and He will help you to attain the level of spiritual growth that will propel you to triumph over all your life challenges.

There are a lot of blessings that come with obeying the word of God and keeping His commandment, and even more in times of difficulty and challenges. (Deuteronomy 28:1-3) says,

"And if you obey the voice of the Lord your God, being careful to do all his

commandments which I commanded you this day, the Lord your God will set you high above all the nations of the earth. And all these blessings shall come upon you and overtake you, if you obey the voice of the Lord your God. Blessed shall you be in the city, and blessed shall you be in the field."

Be Calm And Be Patient

In times of difficult challenges, you need to keep calm and be patient if you desire to overcome it and triumph over it. This is because, when you become frantic and desperate, you resort to very desperate moves that are capable of weighing you down physically, morally and emotionally.

The truth is that the healing we need in times of challenges, and the strength we need to triumph comes only from God, and no other source, so when we are frantic and desperate, we resort to looking for the solution to our challenges in other sources, thereby making the situation worse. If you desire to see victory and triumph over life challenges then you need to be calm and patient and let God take charge of the situation.

Be Joyful And Enjoy Your Life

When the challenges we are facing seems too much to bear, we tend to lose joy in life and we stop to live and enjoy life, but that is a very wrong approach.

This approach will bring nothing but sadness, depression and more challenges. It will keep us in a perpetual state of hopelessness, and rob us of the desire to pray to God, thereby delaying our triumph over our challenges.

A lot of people with challenges tend to wait till the problem is over before they are happy again, but this is wrong. Understand this: the life you are living right now is not your own, neither do you have control over it, so the best time to be joyful and enjoy your life is now.

When you smile and remain joyful no matter the challenge you are going through, and when you enjoy your life in any opportunity that you have even when your situation dictates otherwise, you eliminate despair, depression and sadness, and you develop the strength, motivation and joy to face your challenges, overcome it and become triumphant.

Focus On The Positive Things In Your Life

Despite how difficult the challenge in our life is, there are still some positive things left, though they might not be too noticeable to you because of the pain and difficulty you are going through, but they are there.

And to regain the strength and motivation you need to triumph over the challenges in your life, you need to focus on the good things that are left, and stop dwelling on the challenge, or what you have lost due to the challenge you are going through.

It is common for us to focus more on the difficult part of the challenge, but that is a very wrong approach, because if you don't focus on the good things that you have in times of challenges, you can't appreciate and thank God for all He is doing in your life. And it is by thanking God that the healing and strength to triumph over difficult challenges will materialize.

Focus on the positive things in your life, and thank God for the numerous blessings in your life. That you are even alive and seeking for solution to your challenge is a blessing from God, because the dead does not seek for solution to their problems.

One of the things that makes us not to focus on the positive and good things in our life when we are going through challenge in life is that we try to compare ourselves with others and wish we are like them, but we should realize that everyone has one challenge or the other, and that you are not seeing the challenge does not mean is not there.

Therefore, if you desire to triumph over the challenge in your life, you have to see yourself as special and unique, then start focusing on the good things in your life, appreciate the blessings in your life, thank God for those blessings and ask Him to come into your life to take the burden and pain of that challenge away and give you the strength to triumph over it.

Don't Neglect Your Health

Most times when the challenges in our lives become unbearable and overwhelming, we tend to stop taking care for ourselves and our health. This happens due to the state of complete hopelessness in our situation, but this is wrong.

Being so consumed by the pain and difficulty of the challenge that you are facing so much that you neglect to take adequate care of your health will only worsen the situation and even kill you if you don't immediately reverse that wrong approach.

You need to eat well and balanced diet, eat meals that will supply you the nutrient that will give you strength you need to carry on and wait on the Lord, while he heals you and give you the strength to triumph over you challenge. Also sleep well. Yes, in times of challenges we need to, as a matter of spiritual connection to God, fast always, but we should be wise enough to differentiate between fasting and starving.

Things That Can Block The Move Of God In Your Life And Make You Not To Triumph Over Your Challenges

- **Resistant To God And His Promises**

Sometimes, when the challenge you are facing has lasted so long, and the pain has consumed and overwhelmed our body, soul and spirit, we tend to believe that God has abandoned us, or we start to question His power and existence in the first place.

We ask ourselves,

> *"Why am I going through this much pain and challenge if God truly exists. And if He loves me like the Bible says, then why would He allow so much pain and challenge to affect my life for so long?"*

At this time there will be nothing anyone will tell you about God that you will accept. You stop believing in God and all His promises concerning your life and situation. This approach is costly and counterproductive. God has not forsaken you, but with this mentality, you will delay, or even foreclose, the move of God in your life which will make you not to achieve victory and triumph over your challenges.

The way to overcome your resistance to God and His promises is to totally submit to the will of God no matter how painful your situation is and how long you have suffered because of your challenge.

Be grateful and welcome the will of God in your life. Faithfully commit your life into God's hand and in due time His power will manifest and you will triumph over that challenge.

- **Arrogance**

Arrogant and self-centered people believe that they have all the answers to their problems, or they can get the help they need from other sources without factoring the power of God into the equation.

The Bible says in (1 Samuel 2:3),

"Talk no more so proudly, let no arrogance come from your mouth; for the Lord is a God of knowledge, and by him actions are weighed."

This arrogant mindset hinders the move of God, and deprives us from accessing all that God has in stock for us, even His divine plan to heal us and strengthen us in order to triumph over our challenges. The way to turn around our arrogance and open the door for God to come into our life and fulfill His promise concerning the situation we are facing is to humbly submit to God.

In (1 Peter 5:6-7) the Bible says,

"Humble yourselves therefore under the mighty hand of God, that in due time he may exalt you. Cast all your anxiety on him, for he cares for you."

- **Anger And Resentment**

A lot of people going difficult challenges carry the garbage of anger and resentment with them. That is because someone has either hurt them in the past, or caused their present challenge.

It is OK to get angry at something or someone in your life, maybe that person has hurt you so deeply, and your mind tells you that your anger with the person is justified and right. That's fine, at first. But as a child of God that wants to receive the healing and restoration of God and triumph over your challenges, you need to let go of that anger, bitterness and resentment in order to open the way for God's blessing to come in, because God can't operate in such an atmosphere.

To let go of that anger, bitterness and resentment, forgive whoever has hurt you, or caused you any problem that brought a challenge into your life. It might not be too easy to forgive, especially when the feeling of anger and resentment is deep, and the hurt is much, but you should know that forgiveness is not only for the person that has hurt you, but for yourself also, because without forgiveness you can't really be free from the bitterness you feel and you can't access God's blessing which is the only guaranteed way to triumph over your life challenges.

If you are seeking the face of God, praying and fasting for God to heal you and give you the grace to triumph over your challenges, but you are still holding on to anger, bitterness and resentment, refusing to forgive anyone that has hurt you, then you need to stop wasting your time praying and fasting because God will not respond.

In (Mark 11:25) it is written,

"And whenever you stand praying, forgive, if you have anything against anyone, so that your Father also who is in heaven may forgive you your trespasses."

Also in (Ephesians 4:13) the bible says,

"Let all bitterness and wrath and anger and clamor and slander be put away from you, along with malice."

Anger gives the devil opportunity to come into your life, build a stronghold and dwell there, thereby making all your prayers ineffective. Bitterness makes the devil the controller of your life, and when he is in control, no good thing will come into your life. So, resist him by forgiving whoever has hurt you and rebuke him out of your life in the name of Jesus.

In (Ephesians 4:26-27) the bible says,

"Be angry, but do not sin; do not let the sun go down on your anger, and give no opportunity to the devil."

- **Sin**

Sin is another thing that can hinder you from not triumphing over your challenges.

Consequently, if you desire to be victorious and triumph over the situation in your life, you have to first accept Jesus as your personal Lord and Savior, accept and believe that He died for you on the cross of Calvary to redeem you from your sin, and then start serving God in spirit and in truth.

Sin builds a barrier between you and God, and prevents the Holy Spirit from coming into your life to dwell in order to comfort you in times of challenge.

In (Isaiah 59:1-2) the Bible says,

"Behold, the Lord's hand is not shortened, that it can't save, or his ear dull, that it can't hear; but your iniquities has made a separation between you and your God, and your sins have hidden his face from you so that he does not hear."

Abhor sin today, hate it and run away from it, and you will open the door of your heart for the Holy Spirit of the Lord to dwell in.

Prayer Points

Father, in (Deuteronomy 31:6) your word says,

"Be strong and of good courage, do not fear or be in dread of them; for it is the Lord who goes with you, he will not fail you or forsake you."

Father, I believe that you will not leave me nor forsake me, and I thank you for going before me and giving the strength to triumph over all my life challenges in Jesus name. Amen.

Father, you said in (Jeremiah 32:27) that,

"Behold, I am the Lord, the God of all flesh, is anything too hard for me?"

Father, King of glory, the I am that I am, there is nothing too hard for you to do, so I commit all the challenges I am facing into your able hand, believing that victory is guaranteed and that I will come out triumphant in Jesus name. Amen.

It is written in (Deuteronomy 28:1) that,

"If you obey the voice of the Lord your God, being careful to do all the commandments which I commanded you

***this day, the Lord your God will set you
high above all the nations of the earth."***

Father, I know that it is in keeping your law and commandment shall I receive the grace to triumph over the challenges in my life. So I pray for the wisdom to do your will and live according to your precept in Jesus name. Amen.

It is written in (1 Samuel 2:3),

***"Talk no more so proudly, let no
arrogance come from your mouth; for the
Lord is a God of knowledge, and by him
actions are weighed."***

So Father, any form of arrogance, or negative sinful words that will make me to lose your love and presence, and hinder me from triumphing over the challenges I am facing, I rebuke and reject such acts and words in Jesus name. Amen.

Father, your word says in (1 Peter 5:6-7),

***"Humble yourselves therefore under the
mighty hand of God, that in due time he***

may exalt you. Cast all your anxiety on him, for he cares for you."

Father, I humble myself before you today, I cast all my burdens and challenges into your able hand, and I set myself free of all negative situations in my life, I declare in faith that I am free in Jesus name. Amen.

It is written in (Mark 11:25) that,

"Whenever you stand praying, forgive, if you have anything against anyone, so that your Father also who is in heaven may forgive you your trespasses."

So Father, I pray for your forgiveness over all forms of anger and malice that is hindering me from accessing the needed grace from you to triumph over the challenges in my life. Forgive me Father and set me free in Jesus name. Amen.

In (Ephesians 4:26-27) the bible says,

"Be angry, but do not sin; do not let the sun go down on your anger, and give no opportunity to the devil."

So Father, I pray that any form of sin, any form of anger, hatred that will make me give room and opportunity to the devil to operate in my life, remove it from my life and destroy it by fire in Jesus name. Amen

In (Isaiah 59:1-2) it is written,

"Behold, the Lord's hand is not shortened, that it can't save, or his ear dull, that it can't hear; but your iniquities has made a separation between you and your God and your sins has hidden his face from you so that he does not hear."

Father, I am a sinner, and I believe and accept today that Christ died on the cross to save me. Forgive me all my sins and hear my prayers when I cry to you for help, save me and lead me to triumph over any challenge that has taken away joy from my life in Jesus name. Amen.

Father, people normally say that,

"If there is a man to pray, then there is a God to answer."

So Father, I am making all my prayer in faith, knowing that you are a God that answers prayers. Thank you for answering all my prayers in Jesus name. Amen.

Chapter 10: Dealing With Worry And Anxiety

Worry and anxiety have become part of our lives. And because of the nature of the world we live, these issues will keep arising. Knowing how to deal with it effectively, therefore, is key.

The Bible admonishes us not to worry as God's children. (Psalms 46:10) says,

"Be still and know that I am God, I am exalted among the nations, I am exalted in the earth."

However, despite this command from God, a lot of people still engage in this negative and devastating habit, even the children of God who ought to know better. The best way to handle this negative habit and effectively deal with it is to first know that God is your source of joy and provision and that only Him has the capacity to take away your worry and anxiety.

The Bible says in (1 Peter 5:7),

"Cast all your anxiety on him, for he cares for you."

So, stop worrying and start trusting in God to replace your worry with joy, in fact God is asking you to put all those burdens causing you to worry and have anxiety on him.

Effective Ways To Deal With Worry And Anxiety

- **First You Need To Recognize The Fact That Worry And Anxiety Do Not Solve The Problem**

  Worry and anxiety will only weigh you down, demoralise you and take away your joy, they will not in any way help you out of the problem you are actually facing.

  ### *"Anxiety in a man's heart weighs him down, but a good word makes him glad." - (Proverbs 12:25)*

  There is no single benefit to be gained from worrying, but rather it will bring you more harm spiritually and physically by destroying your health. Health hazards such as high blood pressure, depression, immune system destabilization and chronic insomnia are associated to worry and anxiety.

Also, worry and anxiety are time killers. They rob you of valuable time to do meaningful and progressive work. It is very important for us to differentiate between genuine concern and worry and anxiety. While genuine concern for a situation helps you remain focused, gives you direction and motivation to handle a situation, worry incapacitates you, and robs you of the required focus and motivation you need to face your situation.

You, therefore, need to relax and identify the things or the areas in your life where worry and anxiety are depriving you of the needed focus and motivation to move your life forward and deal with them with help of God.

- **Entrust All Your Worry And Anxiety On God**

Now that you have recognized that worry and anxiety will not help you or change the situation that you are facing, but will rather worsen it by demoralizing and weighing you down, you need to put all your trust in God and let Him take charge of whatever is causing you worry and anxiety.

In (Mathew 11:28), the word of the Lord says,

> ***"Come to me, all who labor and heavy laden, and I will give you rest."***

The solution to your problem does not lie with you, or how well and how long the worry and anxiety lasts, but on God who has the capacity to do all things and to make a way where there is no way.

Know that God desires the best for you at all times, and that he is constantly seeking ways to bless you and expand you, so commit everything in His able care and He will replace your worry with joy and your anxiety with shout of praise.

God's word said in (Jeremiah 29:11),

"For I know the plans I have for you, says the Lord, plans for welfare and not for evil, to give you a future and a hope."

- **Position Your Mind To Think Positive And Edifying Thoughts**

Thoughts are very powerful tools that we can use to improve, motivate and make our lives better or to discourage or depress ourselves. It all depends on how we choose to apply it.

The way we think and what comes out of the soul of a man defines what that man will ultimately become. It is written that, "

As he thinketh in his heart, so he is."
- (Proverbs 23:7)

If our aim is to effectively deal and eliminate worry and anxiety from our lives, then we should make it a point of priority to focus our minds on the positive things in our life and forget the negative things that steal your joy and happiness and leave us hopelessly depressed.

Think of what God has done in your life, what you have been able to accomplish through His help. Yes, it might not be going the way you planned or expected it to happen, but remember that a lot of people died today and all their dreams and aspiration died with them, but you are alive today and there is hope for a better and greater tomorrow. That alone is enough to thank God and give praise to His Holy name.

"Count your blessings, name them one by one and it will surprise you what God has done for you."

In (Philippians 4:8), the Bible tells us the great importance attached to the way we think when it says, "Finally brethren, whatsoever things are true, whatsoever things are honest, whatsoever things are just, whatsoever things are pure, whatsoever things are lovely, whatsoever things are of good report, if there be any virtue, if there be any praise, think on these things."

• Ask God To Give You Peace Of Mind

When the troubles of life become too much for you, and you are completely overwhelmed by the crisis of life.

When you have done everything within your power to deal with the worry and anxiety that is devastating your life, but all efforts have failed, then it is time to go to your Redeemer, go to God and ask Him to give you peace of mind.

God is the only one who can give you the peace of mind to completely deal with worry and anxiety. Medications can't help you, neither will alcohol and narcotics, but only God who created you and knew you from the beginning that can help you.

In (Philippians 4:7) the Bible says,

"And the peace of God, which passes all understanding, will keep your hearts and your mind in Christ Jesus."

When Jesus was on earth, He knew how the heart of man is prone to worry and anxiety, so He told His disciples that He will send a Comforter for them. Without that Comforter, they wouldn't be able to withstand the trials and temptations that will come their way.

"But the Comforter, which is the Holy Ghost, whom the Father will send in my name, he shall teach you all things, and bring all things to your remembrance, whatsoever I said to you, peace I leave with you, my peace I give unto you; not as the world give, give I unto you. Let not

your heart be troubled, neither let it be afraid." - (John 14:26-27)

When trouble becomes too much for us to bear and carry alone, we should ask God to send us the Holy Spirit to comfort and help us bear our burdens.

- **Totally Rely On The Strength Of God**

The truth is that you can't handle your problems alone; neither do you have the capacity as a man to solve all the problems that are causing you worry and anxiety. So, quit trying to handle it all alone and start relying on God's strength to overcome the troubles of life.

In (Psalms 27:1-3) it is written,

"The Lord is my light and my salvation, whom shall I fear? The Lord is the strength of my life; of whom shall I be afraid? When the wicked, even my enemies and my foes, came upon me to eat up my flesh, they stumbled and fell. Though

a host should encamp against me, my heart shall not fear; though war arises against me, in this I shall be confident."

The cause of worry and anxiety is fear, but when we totally rely on the strength of God, we have nothing to fear and worry about, even though the troubles of this world come in different ways and patterns, and our enemies try to create crisis in our life, we are confident that we will come out stronger and victorious, because we rely on the strength of God and not our own strength.

We should also rely on God's promises in times of trouble; because we know that His promises never fail. One of His promises which we can rely on is found on (Isaiah 41:10), which reads,

"Fear not; for I am with thee; be not dismayed; for I am thy God: I will strengthen thee; yea, I will help thee;

yea, I will uphold thee with the right hand of my righteousness."

- **God Is Your Source Of Supply**

Most times we worry and become anxious about our situation because we forget that all that we have is not by our own making. God is the source of our supplies.

The Bible tells us in (James 1:17) that,

"Every good endowment and every perfect gift is from above, coming down from the Father of lights in whom there is no variation or shadow due to change."

God is our source and He gives us all good and perfect gifts of finance, health, wealth, marital success and all our heart desire, so when something goes wrong in our lives, we should go back to our source and He will make everything good again.

Our God and source of all provisions truly loves and cares for us, and He is ever willing to take away those crises and troubles in our lives that cause worry and anxiety and replace them with abundant blessings, joy and happiness.

Sometimes, our lack of faith and trust in the ways and promise of God is why we run from pillar to post, seeking for solutions. And when those places fail us, worry and anxiety set in. If you truly desire to enjoy a life of abundant blessings, joy and happiness and life devoid of worry and anxiety, you have to, as a matter of urgency, connect back to your source (God).

- **Live A Life Of Thanksgiving**

A thankful heart knows no worry! The Bible advises us to give thanks in all situations we find ourselves, and if we abide by this great advice, we will worry less and use our time in giving thanks to God for all He has done for us.

We should make it a priority to start our day with thanksgiving and end it with thanksgiving. Thank God for all the good things He has done in your life, and all that He is about to do. Thank God for letting you see a new day, for the air you breath, the food that you eat, and for all the times He saved you from calamities that you were not even aware of.

The truth is that, thanking God and telling Him all that He has done for you is not reminding God about what He did for you in the present and past, but it is to remind you that the God you serve is capable, willing and in control of everything.

The Bible says,

"All things work for good for those that love the Lord and are called according to his purpose." - (Romans 8:28)

Isn't that enough reason to give thanks to God at all times and in any situation? When you are sure that at the end, God will make that situation you are passing through now a point of blessing and increase in your life.

Thanksgiving enables you to effectively deal with worry and anxiety, and restores hope, peace and joy into your life. In (Philippians 4:6) the Bible tells us,

"Do not be anxious about anything, but in every situation, by prayer and supplication, with thanksgiving, let your request be made known unto God."

The importance of thanksgiving cannot be over emphasized. Learn to praise the Lord at all times and in everything. I love the way Psalm 150 talks about praising God, it says,

"Praise the Lord! Praise God in His sanctuary; praise Him in His mighty firmament, Praise Him for His mighty deeds; praise Him according to His exceeding greatness. Praise Him with trumpet sound; praise Him with lute and harp. Praise Him with

timbrel and dance; praise Him with strings and pipes. Praise Him with sounding cymbals; praise Him with loud clashing cymbals. Let everything that breathes praise the Lord. Praise the Lord!"

This chapter of the Bible makes us know that we have a lot of reasons to thank and to praise the Lord, and we need to praise Him with everything that we have.

For the fact that He gave us life and we can breathe is enough reason to break out in praise and thanksgiving, and of a truth a thankful soul will never suffer worry and anxiety.

- **Live A Life Of Prayer And Faith**

Lack of hope, purpose and direction are some of the reasons why people suffer from worry and anxiety, and this is because, they want to do things their way, or solve their problems without inputting the God factor.

And when they fail, they become worried and anxiety takes over their life.

The truth is that, inputting the God factor in anything that you do positions you for success and there is no better way to put it than how it is said in (Proverbs 3:5-6),

"Trust in the Lord with all your heart, and lean not on your own understanding, in all your ways acknowledge Him, and He shall direct your paths"

If you desire a life that is free from worry and anxiety, and you want to achieve success in all that you do, then you need to pray to God to give you wisdom, direction and understanding. Stop leaning and relying on your own understanding and ask God to direct your paths.

Live a life of faith believing that God has you covered, and that the life you live is not your own, but God's to control and take care of. In (Galatians 2:20), it is written,

> ***"I have been crucified with Christ, it is no longer I who live, but Christ who lives in me; and the life I now live in the flesh, I live by faith in the Son of God, who loved me and gave himself for me."***

As a child of God, you are not in charge of your life or your daily provisions, but God, who loved you and sent His only begotten Son to die for your sins, is in control.

Stop worrying and kill that anxiety in your life and put your faith in God to come through for you because only Him knows your true heart desire and He will surely bring all of it to pass.

So, if you are still worried and anxious, go to God in prayer and He will give you the peace of mind that you need to rest. For His word says,

> ***"Come to me, all who labor and heavy laden, and I will give you rest." - (Mathew 11:28)***

And in (Philippians 4:6-7), the power of prayer to serve as an antidote to worry and anxiety is emphasized when it says,

> ***"Have no anxiety about anything, but in everything by prayer and supplication with thanks giving let your request be made known to God. And the peace of God, which passes all understanding, will keep your hearts and minds in Christ Jesus."***

Prayer is the key to overcoming worry and anxiety, and prayer done with supplication and thanksgiving will give you the peace of mind you need to overcome worry and anxiety.

• Ask For God's Help To Defeat Bad Habits

The truth is that the unhealthy way some live their life makes them prone to worry and anxiety. Although they may have crisis and trouble in their lives, it is not always the cause.

Someone who has developed the bad and unhealthy habit of turning to alcohol, narcotics intake or other harmful substances when faced with a little problem, rather than turn to God for help will always be prone to worry and anxiety.

To deal with worry and anxiety effectively, you need to ask God for help in dealing with the harmful bad habits and start living a healthy lifestyle. Our health and state of mind affects us in a lot of ways, so we need to start eating healthy foods, drink a lot of clean water and sleep well in order to avoid worry and anxiety.

Prayer Points

Father, you said in (Psalms 46:10) that I should,

"Be still and know that I am God, I am exalted among the nations, I am exalted in the earth."

Father, you are God that is greater than all other gods, you are God that gives peace and prosperity, I beg you for the peace of mind to be still and calm over all the forms of worry and anxiety in Jesus name. Amen.

It is written in (1 Peter 5:7),

"Cast all your anxiety on him, for he cares for you."

So Father, in the name of your Son Jesus Christ, I cast all my worry, fears and anxiety into your able hands, and I know that all my problems are solved because you care for me. Thank you Father, in Jesus name I pray. Amen.

Father, your word says,

"Anxiety in a man's heart weighs him down, but a good word makes him glad." - (Proverbs 12:25)

So Father, I humbly ask today in faith for you to kill all forms of anxiety and worry in my life, and replace it with gladness and peace of mind in Jesus name. Amen.

Father, your word says in (Jeremiah 29:11),

"For I know the plans I have for you, says the Lord, plans for welfare and not for evil, to give you a future and a hope."

So Father, by the power of the Holy Ghost I banish every form of hopelessness and failure that is bringing me worry and anxiety, and I key into the glorious plan welfare, hope and a great future that you have for me in Jesus name. Amen.

It is written that,

"As he thinks in his heart, so he is." - (Proverbs 23:7)

Father, by the blood of Jesus I come against any negative mindset that is bringing me fear, worry and anxiety, and plead for your wisdom and understanding to be positive minded and achieve greatness in Jesus name. Amen.

"But the comforter, which is the Holy Ghost, whom the father will send in my name, he shall teach you all things, and bring all things to your remembrance, whatsoever I said to you, peace I leave with you, my peace I give unto you; not as

the world give, give I unto you. Let not your heart be troubled, neither let it be afraid." - (John 14:26-27)

Father, in (Isaiah 41:10) you said,

"Fear not; for I am with thee, be not dismayed; for I am thy God: I will strengthen thee; yea, I will help thee; yea, I will uphold thee with the right hand of my righteousness."

So Father, today I put away fear and I start walking in faith for you are with me and I have nothing to fear or worry about.

Thank you Father, in Jesus name, Amen.

It is written that,

"All things work for good for those that love the Lord and are called according to his purpose." - (Romans 8:28)

Father, I thank you for the situation in my life, I thank you for you are bigger than the situation. I refuse to be worried and be anxious over the situation because I know that with you, the situation will turn to good and praise, honor and glory will be to your Holy name in Jesus name. Amen.

Father, you said,

"Come to me, all who labor and heavy laden, and I will give you rest." - (Mathew 11:28)

Father, only you are the true giver of rest, the giver of joy and peace. So today I put all the heavy problems, the burdens and pains that have made my life filled with worry and anxiety and I run into your rest in Jesus name. Amen.

Father, your word says in (Philippians 4:6-7),

"Have no anxiety about anything, but in everything by prayer and supplication with thanks giving let your request be made known to God. And the peace of God, which passes all understanding, will keep your hearts and minds in Christ Jesus."

Thank you Father, for I reject to have worry and anxiety over anything, but instead I will give you praise and thank you for all you have done for me. Thank you for your mercy and provision in Jesus name I pray. Amen.

Chapter 11: Victory Is Certain In Christ Jesus

As a child of God, you will experience trials and tribulations, and adversities of different forms might come your way, but there is none of them that God cannot deliver you from and make you come out victorious!

Jesus Himself gave us assurance of this victory we will enjoy as His followers when He said,

"I have said this to you, that in me you may have peace, in the world you have tribulation, but be of good cheer, I have overcome the world." - (Luke 16:33)

Jesus is not only giving us assurance of the victory that is already ours in His name, but He goes further to say we should 'be of good cheer', that is, to start rejoicing and be happy because your victory is certain and confirmed.

When Jesus was crucified on the cross, before He gave up the ghost, He said,

"It is finished." - (John 19:30)

It means your problems are finished. The challenges that have held you captive and made your life worthless and meaningless have been taken care of, the solutions to all your worry and anxiety have been found, so rejoice and be glad because your victory has been signed, sealed and delivered into your hand by the victory of Jesus on the cross.

God is always with you, the assurance of the victory that is yours has already been promised by God when He said,

"When you pass through the waters, I will be with you; and through the rivers, they shall not overflow you. When you walk through the fire, you shall not be burned, nor shall the flame scorch you." - (Isaiah 43:2)

In this verse in Isaiah, the word of God is saying that due to the nature of the fallen and sinful world that we are living in, we are bound to have problems and challenges, but through Him, and also through the price that Jesus paid on the cross of Calvary our victory is certain and assured.

In (1 Corinthians 15:57), the Bible says,

"But thanks be to God, which gives us the victory through our Lord Jesus Christ."

For everyone that is a child of God, and believes in the resurrection power of Jesus Christ, victory over life challenge is a certainty it does not matter how difficult that challenge, and how long you have suffered on that challenge, the power in the blood of Jesus, to wash away sins, to heal and restore is available for you to overcome life challenges and come out victorious.

In (1 John 5:4-5) the Bible says that,

"For whatever is born of God overcomes the world; and this is the victory that overcomes the world, our faith. Who is he that overcomes the world but he who believes that Jesus is the son of God."

The moment you realize who you are in Christ and the power inherent in the blood of Jesus, you will realize the power that God has deposited in you to conquer every evil, and every challenge that comes your way.

The bible says,

"Behold, I have given you authority to tread upon serpents and scorpions, and over all the power of the enemy, and nothing shall hurt you." - (Luke 10:19)

To have victory in Christ Jesus requires that you totally surrender your life to Christ and let the will of God be supreme over your own will. Your spirit, soul and body should come in alliance with the will of God for your life in order to be free from the shackles of sin, sickness and challenges and enjoy the victory that is certain in Jesus.

In (1 Corinthians 15:54-57) the Bible says,

"When the perishable puts on the imperishable, and the mortal puts on the immortality, then shall come to pass the saying that is written 'Death is swallowed up in victory, O death, where is thy victory? O death where is thy sting? The

sting of death is sin, and the power of sin is the law.' But thanks be to God, who gave us the victory through our Lord Jesus Christ."

Victory is certain in Christ Jesus, that's only if you forsake sin and completely submit to God. The will of God is for every of His creature to come under the Lordship of Jesus Christ.

Hence, the Bible says in (Philippians 2:9-11),

"Therefore God has highly exalted him and bestowed on Him the name which is above all names, that at the name of Jesus every knee should bow, in heaven and on earth and under the earth, and every tongue confess that Jesus Christ is Lord, to the glory of God the Father."

Victory in the name of Jesus can only be gotten when the restorative power of the blood of Jesus restores all things to the way God designed it to be from the beginning. Because in the beginning, God created everything perfect - without sin, without sickness, without problems and challenges. But sin entered into the picture and changed everything, bringing with it all the problems that man is going through today. This is why it was important for God to send His son to die on the cross for us and make everything right again.

In (John 3:16-18) it is written,

> *"For God so loved the world that he gave his only Son, that whoever believes in him should not perish but have eternal life, for God sent the Son into the world, not to condemn the world, but that the world might be saved through him. He who believes in him is not condemned; he who does not believe is condemned already, because he has not believed in the name of the only Son of God."*

The good news about this is that the sickness, marital challenge, financial challenge and every other mental, physical and psychological challenge that you are going through, have all been nailed to the cross of Calvary. Christ had defeated all your challenges and your victory and freedom is guaranteed.

Knowing our identity in Christ Jesus is the surest way to achieve victory over our life challenges, because if you don't know and understand this, there is no way that you can access or key into that power to work in your situation.

The Bible says,

"My people perish for lack of knowledge."
- (Hosea 4:6)

When we get the knowledge of who we are in Christ, then no matter the degree of difficulty and challenge that we encounter, we will remain in God, cheerful because Christ has overcome the world for us.

The identity we have in Christ removes the fear of being crushed by the challenges we face in this world. It also gives us the faith that our redemption and victory is certain in Christ Jesus. It emboldens us to believe that we can overcome the instability and hopelessness in this world.

In (Romans 8:14-15), the Bible says,

> **"For all who are led by the spirit of God are the sons of God, for you did not receive the spirit of slavery to fall back into fear, but you have received the spirit of son-ship, when we cry Abba Father."**

Once you receive Christ as your personal Lord and savior, you begin to live in faith, and the fear of financial challenges, the fear of health, marital, spiritual, job loss and other forms of challenges will be eliminated and replaced with the certainty of the victory that Jesus procured for us on the cross of Calvary when he said, *"It Is Finished."*

As it is written in (2 Corinthians) that,

> **"Therefore, if anyone is in Christ, he is a new creation, the old has passed away, behold the new has come."**

Now that we are in Christ Jesus, we have become overcomers in everything and over all life's challenges, because the Christ we are connected to and that redeemed us with His blood has overcome all things. So our spirit, soul and body are now hidden in Jesus with God. No challenge, obstacle and manipulation of the evil ones can penetrate us.

Christ has bought us with a price, and our new identity is in Him, we are now enveloped by the grace of God. We now have access to the name of Jesus as our weapon to overcome all the evil plans of the enemy. For the Bible says in (Revelation 12:11),

"And they have conquered him by the blood of the lamb and by the word of their testimony."

When you have fought the battles of life and won, then it is time to praise the name of the Lord and to live a life of faith knowing that the God you serve is well able to fight all your battles and give you victory for the glory of His Holy name.

There Is Light At The End Of The Tunnel

Whatever we are going through, no matter how painful and difficult the situation is, we should know that it has an expiring date. Truth is, there is light at the end of the tunnel.

But while in the tunnel, we need to have an attitude of faith in order to be able to emerge from the tunnel victorious.

The tunnel in our life depicts the challenges, the troubles and trials that sometimes characterize our life.

While in the tunnel, we need to seek a way out in order to see the light again. And the only way we need to seek in order to see the light again, is to first give our life to Jesus Christ, and then make Him the Lord and savior of our life.

For the Bible says in (John 8:12),

"I am the light of the world, he who follows me will not walk in darkness, but will have the light of life."

Therefore, seek to follow Jesus every day in works, actions, thoughts and speeches, and your light will break forth to light up the tunnel in your life.

In (Proverbs 23:18) the Bible says,

"For surely there is an end; and thy expectation shall not be cut off."

So no matter what you are going through right now, hold on strongly to God in faith for there will surely be an end to that situation and all your expectations in life will be fulfilled.

Prayer Points

It is written in (Luke 16:33) that,

"I have said this to you, that in me you may have peace, in the world you have tribulation, but be of good cheer, I have overcome the world."

Father, I receive the peace that only you can give, today and forever give me the grace to be in good cheer for Christ has overcome all my struggles and challenges and I am free in Jesus name. Amen.

Jesus, you said in your word that,

"It is finished" - (John 19:30)

So Father, I decree and declare that all the pains, difficulties and challenges that I am facing in life is finished forever in Jesus name. Amen.

Father, you said in your word that,

"When you pass through the waters, I will be with you; and through the rivers, they shall not overflow you. When you walk through the fire, you shall not be burned, nor shall the flame scorch you." - (Isaiah 43:2)

Father, I believe in your promises , and banish any contrary voice that is saying otherwise in my life and holding me back from enjoy the victory that Christ has made certain in my life in Jesus name. Amen.

It is written In (1 Corinthians 15:57) that,

"But thanks be to God, which gives us the victory through our Lord Jesus Christ."

Father, I give you thanks for the victory that you have given me over all challenges in my life through Christ Jesus. Thank you for this victory is certain and guaranteed in Jesus name. Amen.

It is written in (1 John 5:4) that,

"For whatever is born of God overcomes the world; and this is the victory that overcomes the world, our faith."

Father, I pray for the faith to hold on strongly to you and your promises even in the face of trials and tribulations for I know that through faith I shall overcome everything that comes my way and enjoy victory in Jesus name. Amen.

Father, you said that,

"Behold, I have given you authority to tread upon serpents and scorpions, and over all the power of the enemy, and nothing shall hurt you." - (Luke 10:19)

So Father, with the authority that you have given me, I decree that I have obtained victory over any form of attack and spiritual manipulations in my life in Jesus name. Amen.

It is written that,

"My people perish for lack of knowledge."
- (Hosea 4:6)

So Father, I pray in the name of Jesus for you to give me wisdom and open my eyes of understanding to know the power you have given me to overcome my challenges and come out victorious in Jesus name. Amen.

It is written in (2 Corinthians 5:17) that,

"Therefore, if anyone is in Christ, he is a new creation, the old has passed away, behold the new has come."

So Father, I receive my newness in Christ Jesus, and I declare that all the old things in my life that brought me pains, struggles and problems are hereby replaced with the joy of victory in Christ Jesus. Amen.

It is written,

"And they have conquered him by the blood of the lamb and by the word of their testimony." - (Revelation 12:11)

Father, today in the name of Jesus I conquer all the adversity, the challenges and every negative thing in my life by the blood of the lamb and the words of my testimony in Jesus name. Amen.

Conclusion

The life of man is characterized by ups and downs. There is no certainty and permanency to anything in life. The only place where we can find stability, peace and strength to go through all the daily challenge that we face in life in Jesus Christ.

This is why Jesus said in (John 16:33),

"These things I have spoken unto you, that in me you might have peace. In the world you shall have tribulation; but be of good cheer; I have overcome the world."

So, be of good cheer, your Lord Jesus has overcome the world. He lost His life so you can live your own life to the fullest. Don't allow worry and anxiety steal your peace, kill your passion and destroy your life. It shall end in praise in Jesus' name.

THE AUTHOR

Wale Oyeniyi is a man of many parts. He is a Teacher, a gifted Author, a Preacher, an Educationist, a Philanthropist, and an Entrepreneur.

An Alumnus of Obafemi Awolowo University (OAU), The Redeemed Christian Church of God Bible College and Haggai Institute, USA. He has attended several leadership courses at home and abroad.

He is a friend and mentor to many people around the world. He is an adherent proponent of leadership by example. He is much sought after as a speaker in churches, seminars, and conferences

He is the President of RightFinder© International, an NGO that amongst other things specialize in organizing seminars, conferences, prayer meetings, counseling, educating Youths, Young Adults, and leaders of businesses and ministers of the Gospel around the world.

He is happily married and enjoying God's best with his family.

NOTES